Beyond Our Control—*Rape*

Beyond Our Control—*Rape*

A Biblical, Historical &

Social Perspective of One of

the Oldest Sins Committed

Against Women

Leila Rae Sommerfeld

A Division of WINEPRESS PUBLISHING

ISBN 1-4141-0478-2
Library of Congress Catalog Card Number: 2005904192

All reasonable attempts were made to discover the origin of 'author unknown' and various other quotes. If you are the author, or know the origin, please let me know so that I may give credit where credit is due.

Dedication

DEDICATED TO

God
and
Women of Courage

To those who have suffered in silence
and are brave enough to trust God for
new wings as He encourages us to fly beyond
tolerable recovery and break free from
strongholds that bind us to the past.

Contents

Acknowledgments

My deep appreciation to ...

Bettie P. Mitchell, L.P.C., M.R., Founder/Director of Good Samaritan Ministries International, Beaverton, Oregon, author of *Who Is My Neighbor?* Thanks for endorsing my book and showing me what it means to be a servant of Jesus Christ.

My sisters Linda Montgomery and Gloria Griggs, my niece Lee Ann Smith, and friends Karen Hill, Ruth Morlock, Lee Ann Dillon, Edna Cooke, and Ruth Hermance for wading though the manuscript in its infancy.

To Bobbie Breedlove for editing the manuscript more times than she cared. Her steadfast encouragement kept me going when at times I felt like a total failure.

To my husband, D.D., for patiently listening to my endless babble and frustrations while birthing the book. I'm sure he is delighted it's finished!

Candace Walters, author of *Invisible Wounds,* for allowing me to reprint an abundance of her writing.

Judy Boen, Prison Chaplain, Grover Beach, California, and Dr. Larry Day, Ph.D., Portland, Oregon, author of *Self Esteem–By God's Design* for graciously endorsing my book.

To all the sexual assault survivors and perpetrators who shared their stories with me.

To those who asked, "How is your book coming along?" and to those whom I have forgotten.

I will bring health and healing; I will heal my people and let them enjoy abundant peace and security.

—Jeremiah 33:6

O Woman of Another Time

O woman of another time, I found thee weeping,
Waiting to be rescued from the terrible evil,
After tasting forbidden fruit, which caused The Fall,
Making the Son die to save us all.

Chains broke at last, thy strongholds of thy past.
O weeping woman, thy legions fled,
Cast into the sea of dead.
Thy accuser, he whom your soul reviled,
The Son of God did trample on,
Endued thee with peace secured with truth
Beneath His wings of love.

Thou kissed with mercy and held by grace,
Someday thou shalt see Him face to face.

—L.R.S.

PART I
BEYOND OUR
CONTROL: RAPE
MY STORY

"IF ONLY WISDOM, IN THE WINTER OF LIFE, COULD HAVE BEEN USED IN THE
SPRING OF YOUTH, HOW DIFFERENT IT MIGHT HAVE BEEN."
—L.R.S.

Dear Reader

On one single night, an intruder tore apart the fabric of my life, leaving me frozen in fear. More than three decades passed in silence before that fear melted.

During the summertime, more than forty years ago, I was raped in my home. My children were asleep in the next room; my husband was out of town. The rapist, I later learned, was a distant neighbor. Our home was isolated, making a prompt rescue impossible.

The grotesque violence of that night left me shattered for years. Unfortunately, I failed to receive the medical, mental, emotional, and spiritual help that could have spared me decades of sorrow. My marriage dissolved, I suffered a mental breakdown, and fear held me hostage. Anxiety, panic attacks, depression, and numerous other dysfunctions followed. As the years passed, I kept asking, "Why?"

Are the narcissistic pleasure seekers who rape, kill, mug, and steal beautiful creatures created in the image of God? Why are people evil? Why does God allow it? Where does the blame lie—with God, Satan, Adam, or Eve? Or with the dogmas of the canon, the traditional church, or modern society?

What do the Scriptures mean about the equality of men and women? Was man's disdain for women passed from generation to generation through his sons?

Some wounded women feel justified in their anger toward men in general. After all, men have never been held in subordination to women. The unspeakable atrocities committed against women and children from the beginning of time have been hideous. Was this sorrow cast upon woman because Eve ate the apple in the Garden of Eden, causing the downfall of humankind?

In order to break free from the strongholds of my past, I needed answers to my questions. My search resulted in a biblical, social, and historical study on the evil of rape and violence toward women.

Digging deep, I learned that God values everyone equally. However, contrary to God's intention, women have been held subservient to men. The distinctions between man and woman appear in the creation stories. One account says woman was created equally with man in God's image, yet another says she was created to meet man's needs.

Angry women have rebelled against the idea of "meeting man's needs," because it makes them feel second rate. Revengeful men have used these Scriptures against women, subjecting them to slavery, mental and emotional abuse, and violence.

This book will present negative information about *abusive* men; however, it is not meant to be a male-bashing book, nor is it intended to nurture bitterness.

Please be assured that I highly admire and respect godly men who love humankind. It brings me great joy to see a father play lovingly with his children. I am touched when a husband puts his arm around his wife and draws her close. To gaze at worshipping man restores trust and faith in my heart.

My traumas (rape, mental illness, divorce, and more) left me with fear, a hardened heart, and a negative attitude; I was on the brink of suicide. I begged God for peace—dead or alive. God heard and responded with an everlasting promise: *"I will bring peace to your life like the calm on the morning pond."*

My journey to wholeness included interaction with perpetrators in an abuse recovery group at Good Samaritan Ministries, a Christian nonprofit mental-health clinic. Many of the perpetrators were ex-convicts on parole. As I listened to their stories, my hatred and disdain toward men turned to forgiveness and compassion.

We are all perpetrators of some kind. We all have errors in our thinking. The degree to which we get well, offend, or re-offend depends on how well we manage our denial and our thoughts. The extent to which we see another person as a fellow human being (empathy) depends on our decision to hold on to unforgiveness and remain a victim or to forgive and live victoriously.

While our pain never comes without a price, our scars can bear witness to God's unfailing love; He can create new life in you. If you are mad at God, or if your heart has hardened toward men or mankind, please read on. You too can find healing and peace in this beautiful, savage world.

Awesome blessings!

—Leila Rae

So I turned my mind to understand, to investigate and to search out wisdom and the scheme of things and to understand the stupidity of wickedness and the madness of folly.

—Ecclesiastes 7:25

The Intruder

How was I to know, before the dawn,
that my life would never be the same,
that the safety I once felt inside my fortress walls
would be shattered like splintered glass,
cutting deep into my soul, leaving mortal pain,
carving fear into my heart?
You, stranger in the night, intruding into my very being,
consuming all my peace, crushing my spirit,
filling me with terror.
I will never be the same.

—L.R.S.

CHAPTER 1

Nighttime Intruder

"Then the evil one from hell sprang out of nowhere, pouncing upon his prey quickly, smoothly, and quietly like a cat stalking its kill."

—L.R.S.

Corona, California, 1963: Summer. John F. Kennedy died that year. I died a little that year too; I was raped. My rape occurred before 9/11, rape crisis centers, and trauma counselors. I didn't dare discuss it with anyone for fear of ridicule, disbelief, shame, and embarrassment. Fear like I had never encountered was my constant shadow, and trust was a word cancelled from my senses.

The stifling heat was cooling down as the end of a beautiful, clear summer day came to a close. It was warm and muggy inside my home, making me feel like a sticky bun. The swamp cooler wheezed damp air around my bare legs as I opened the bedroom windows and checked on our sleeping girls (who were three and six years old). I went to the garage to retrieve a load of dry laundry, took it to the bedroom, and tossed it on the bed. Thirsty for a cool drink, I padded to the kitchen to see what I could find. The blast of cold air from the refrigerator felt delicious as I reached for a soda.

Later, folding clothes in peaceful silence, I let my mind wander aimlessly with thoughts of the coming week.

My husband Jack had gone to Mexico with my father to pick up a car after my stepmother died at a cancer clinic. He was driving the car home and wouldn't be back until after midnight.

Darkness closed in as the clock struck ten.

Without warning, the lights went out.

Okay, Leila, I assured myself. *So the lights went out—don't panic.*

Why do these things always happen when I'm alone?

I got the flashlight and went to check the power box, hoping I wouldn't encounter a tarantula or rattlesnake.

Looking back, I wish that's only what I'd found.

I'd just started for the garage when I thought I heard a noise. I stopped, stood very still, and listened. Maybe it was my imagination. No, there it was again. The familiar sound of feet crunching gravel on our walkway. My heart beat fast as I flew to the telephone and dialed the operator.

"Someone's trying to break into my home. I'm alone with my children. Get me the police. Hurry!"

While I waited on hold, the intruder banged wildly on the front door, then on the back door. Windows rattled and doors shook like vibrating thunder. I trembled with terror. He continued pounding the doors like a wild beast, unconcerned about the noise. Why should he—who would hear it? Dogs barking outside added more noise. I was afraid the girls would wake up.

"Corona police," announced a sleepy voice through the phone.

I quickly told him what was happening.

"I'm sorry, but you're in the county. You'll have to call the sheriff."

"No!" My heart sank.

Why couldn't they put the call through for me? *Dear God, please help!*

The operator had stayed on the line, and she'd heard his reply. So she put me through to the sheriff. I repeated what was happening and tried to give coherent directions to our home, which was hard to locate after dark. No street lights, no sign at the bottom of the hill—just a few landmarks enclosed in the black ink of night.

The sheriff promised to come right over. I knew he wouldn't make it in time—but in time for what? Robbery? Rape? Murder? I laid the phone down without hanging up, though I wasn't sure why, other than it helped me feel connected to the outside world.

Panic set in. I felt defenseless against the unseen enemy. I ran to the bedroom closet and took our gun from the shelf.

"I have a gun, and I'll use it," I shouted at the intruder. My voice sounded weak and unthreatening. "You'd better get out of here. I've called the sheriff."

His erratic banging didn't stop.

I decided to fire a warning shot. The gun felt smooth and cool in my sweating hand as my finger curled around the trigger, drawing it toward me. But nothing happened! I tried again—nothing!

I felt hopeless and helpless. The intruder probably thought I was bluffing. He was in control, and he knew it.

Nighttime Fear

Lord, my body trembles and my heart pounds
as I hear the deafness of the nighttime sounds.
The stillness of the night surrounds me,
passing slowly all alone in the dark,
while waiting for morning and the sight of the sun
and the sound of the meadowlark.
Relief floods my soul; my heart is happy again.
Daytime, warm and bright,
forgetting the fear that comes with the night.
—L.R.S.

Our house sat high on a hill, like a painted lady sunning herself, absorbing heat on her pale yellow, stucco walls. With mountains rising to the south and a 350-degree view, I was able to see for miles. There were rolling hills, valleys, ravines, and acres and acres of orange groves. When the trees were in blossom and the breeze just right, their heavenly scent would float in the air, intoxicating my nostrils.

A few houses dotted the hills below. While I occasionally saw someone wave, I never heard them.

It was a bumpy ordeal getting to the house. The rutted dirt road to our home was about a half mile off a paved service road. In good weather it wasn't too bad; put the car in low gear, point it straight ahead, give it some gas, and up I'd go, lurching and bouncing, leaving dust in the face of anyone brave enough to follow. The hill was steep, making it impossible to see my final destination. I'm sure visitors wondered if they would drop off the summit's edge.

Rainfall was sparse in California, and when it came, it was a deluge. Our road was clay dirt, and trying to slog through mud would cause visitors to walk out of their boots. Usually cars couldn't get up the hill if it was muddy; they would slip and slide like ice cream trying to cling to a tree. Many gave up, parked their car at the bottom and walked. What an experience!

And just try leading tired children, carrying wet bags of groceries while the contents spilled out, and dodging lightning that danced at your feet.

We had frequent power outages. But we didn't mind. Candles, flashlights, and an occasional fire in the fireplace made the outages seem like celebrations. Besides, the power was never off for long.

The drive to town was about eight miles; my parents lived about thirty miles away. I'd wanted horses, and we needed property we could afford. The five-acre parcel, despite its daunting appearance, filled the bill. We'd built a modest house, erected a small barn, put in fences, and planted a few trees and shrubs.

Just to complicate my life a little more, I enrolled at the local junior college and pursued the study of cosmetology. Five days a week, eight hours a day, I endured the jolt of returning to school. I carried the load of keeping the home fires burning and caring for animals, along with the guilt of leaving my girls with after-school sitters.

One year later, after zealous perseverance, I completed my academic studies and was eager to apply my newfound knowledge. However, my new career would have to wait; the most hideous, life-altering experience of my life was about to take place, with an impact that would leave my mind, body, and soul forever changed.

Fear mounted as I stood shaking in the middle of the house. I didn't know what to do except pray.

In the flash of a second, the evil intruder sprang at me from out of nowhere. He yanked my head back by my hair.

His arm flew around my neck, and then he grabbed the gun from my hand.

My free hand swung around, briefly illuminating his face with the flashlight. I did not recognize him.

He threw the gun on the sofa, seized the flashlight, and twisted my arm behind my back. Then he pushed me toward the bedroom and said, "Don't fight, and you won't get hurt."

Did I know this evil man? I wasn't sure. But he apparently knew me; from where?

Please, dear God, don't let the girls get up. I not only feared for their lives; I didn't want this horrible scene etched forever in their memory.

"Take off your clothes," he demanded.

My eyes swelled with tears as I started to unbutton my blouse.

Because I didn't want the girls to hear anything, I offered no resistance to his advances. I did as I was told, though I made no effort to be an obliging participant.

He only spoke to give me orders. He didn't talk at all during the assault. I failed to recognize him or his voice.

As I lay there enduring this monster's attack, the dogs stopped barking. The house became strangely quiet. The silence was broken by one of my daughters shouting, "Mother!"

"It's all right, honey, go back to sleep," I replied through quivering lips, forcing my voice to sound calm. Miraculously, she did as she was told. I wondered if the noise or the silence woke her.

After the assault, the man stood, zipped his pants and said, "Get me your purse!"

Sitting up, my hazy mind drew a blank. "I can't remember where it is."

"Well, you'd better remember, and quick!"

Chapter 1: Nighttime Intruder: Defenseless against the Unseen Enemy

Shivering from cold and shock, I wandered around the house naked with the man trailing behind me. I tried to remember where I'd put my purse, but all I could think about was whether the girls and I would be murdered.

When I finally found the purse, he seized it, and then ran out the back door.

I immediately locked the door, not realizing he had climbed in through a bedroom window. I went to my bedroom, put on a robe, then grabbed a towel from the bathroom and wiped my legs. Frightened that he would return and kill all of us, I got the girls up and made a bed for them in the bathtub. I don't remember the reason I gave them; they just climbed in dutifully and soon fell asleep—another miracle.

Indescribable fear gripped me as I locked the bathroom door and watched out the tiny window for the lights of the sheriff's car, praying he would hurry. I felt like a character in a horror movie. This couldn't be happening to me. It must be a dream. Surely I would wake up soon.

But it wasn't a dream. It was a living nightmare.

Finally, I saw car lights, flashing up and down, back and forth like searchlights. Though I was sure it was the sheriff, I felt apprehensive about opening the front door. How could I be sure it was safe?

I crept to the living room and peered out the window, straining my eyes to make out the figure stepping onto the porch. He held a flashlight in one hand and a gun in the other.

I slowly opened the door, feeling dirty and embarrassed, though I didn't know why. I hadn't done anything wrong.

I wanted to say, "It's too late. I've been raped. What took you so long?"

The sheriff found the power box and flipped a switch that turned on the lights in the house. I felt exposed, like a freak from a sideshow.

Trembling, I let him inside and offered him a seat in the living room. Even though it was warm in the house, I felt cold and sick to my stomach. I wrapped my robe tightly around my body as I sat on the couch. I did my best to describe what had happened. The word *rape* stuck in my throat. Finally, I whispered, "He raped me."

He said I should go to the hospital for an examination and offered to take me.

"My husband is on his way home from Mexico," I explained. "I can't go until he gets here. I can't leave my children alone."

He nodded. "I understand."

"He should be home sometime after midnight."

"I'll wait until he comes home. In the meantime, you can get dressed and take the sheets off of your bed. We'll need them so the crime lab can look for semen. We'll also need the clothes you took off. Oh, and don't wash yourself."

Don't wash myself? I thought. *How long do I have to live with his filth?*

I moved in slow motion, feeling like an outsider observing myself gliding from room to room, collecting evidence for the crime lab.

When my husband Jack finally arrived, after what seemed like an eternity, I tearfully told him what had happened. His expression revealed shock that such a horror could happen in his home.

"If I get hold of that____I'll kill him," he yelled, his face flushing.

I phoned a friend who lived nearby and asked her to stay with the girls while Jack and I went to the hospital. While we waited for her to arrive, I wondered why I hadn't called her when I first heard the attacker. Maybe I couldn't remember her phone number in my panic; perhaps I didn't want to lose the operator; maybe I was just numb with fear.

Chapter 1: Nighttime Intruder: Defenseless against the Unseen Enemy

We went to the hospital emergency room. The lobby was quiet and empty at three A.M. After filling out paperwork, I was whisked into a small examination room and told to undress—again. White protective paper crinkled beneath my body as I climbed onto the examination table, clothed in a skimpy gown. I was alone, with no nurse—no husband—no one to hold my hand. Shiny silver stirrups stared at me, urging my feet to slide in and feel the sensation of cold metal. Shaking, I felt I was about to be raped again.

The examining doctor talked little, his voice devoid of emotion. I spoke only when questioned. In my heart, I begged God to help me get through the whole ordeal.

After the exam, Jack led me back to the car. I curled up tight on the front seat. As we drove home in silence, the sun came up. The sky glowed with a confetti of crimson colors as a sliver of moon was pushed into another night. I hugged a sweater close around my body as if to protect myself from further violence.

I wanted to die. That seemed ironic since, during the rape, I was afraid of being murdered. Did it matter now if I lived when part of me was already dead?

When we got home, I shuffled inside and took a shower. I then crawled into bed, and pulled the covers over my head.

Can I ever stay alone in this house again?

God, how could You allow this to happen?

My husband notified all my family. Nobody came to see me. I wasn't sure I wanted to see them anyway.

A detective came by later that afternoon. He asked a few questions, to see if I could identify my perpetrator. Sitting at the kitchen table, he opened a large book.

"Leila, look at these pictures. Don't rush. Study them closely."

After a lengthy time of viewing the photos, I vaguely recognized one face. After pointing it out, the detective informed me that he was a distant neighbor—one with a long criminal history of sexual abuse charges.

The detective led me to the window and pointed to a house in the valley below. I'd been in that home once, to sell products to the man's mother. I remembered he and his mother acting rather strange, and that he had a little girl about three years old. Poor child.

Who knows what he had done to her?

The detective asked if I'd be willing to take a polygraph test. I was taken aback. Couldn't he see from my shaky emotions that I was telling the truth? Wasn't the rape exam enough?

Feeling more like a criminal than a victim, I said, "Yes." I didn't have anything to hide.

After the detective left, I crawled back into bed and covered my head again. Hiding from the outside world, I wanted only darkness. But every time I tossed and turned, sunlight would peek in, coaxing me to get up.

After the rapist had been arrested, I expected a court hearing would be conducted. When he'd been convicted and sentenced, perhaps then I could rise out of the rubble of my life and piece it back together.

The morning silence was broken by the ringing of the phone. Expending all the energy I could muster, I climbed out of bed and answered it.

"Hello."

"You little tramp!" a shrill voice cackled.

Recoiling instinctively, I suspected this was the strange mother of the rapist.

"Who is this?"

"I know your kind. I saw you at the bar."

I never went to bars!

"Everything you said about my son is a lie. You'd better watch out. And you'd better watch your girls. Leave my son alone, or you'll be sorry!"

Anger welled up inside me. How dare this woman threaten me and my children. I quickly hung up and called the detective. He said he would be out immediately and put a wiretap on the phone.

The menacing phone calls continued day and night. I never knew when one would intrude.

Concerned for my children's safety, I started driving them to and from their school bus stop. Again, I haven't a clue what excuse I gave them.

Everyone who heard about the rape was eager to give me safety advice. My father suggested I buy a guard dog. My stepfather told me to purchase another gun—one without a safety latch. He said, "If you had learned to use the gun properly, the assault might have been prevented," as if it were my fault it took place. Discussing the trauma with my mother was out of the question. She was perpetually nervous, and would be of no help.

I knew they were all trying to be helpful. But they weren't. Their comments only poured more stress into my overloaded mind. My family had no idea of the seriousness of my mental state, nor did they perceive the depth of my trauma. It was more than the rape. The fear leading up to the assault was overwhelming—fear for me, and more so, fear for my children's safety. I needed love, comfort, and support, not a checklist for dealing with would-be intruders.

Vivid, ugly nightmares started appearing night after night, over and over again. Like a fast-forward movie, each scene would play out the same powerful message: hunt her down, chase her fast, hurt her bad, and terrify her. It wasn't just one man climbing up the hill to attack me; it was an army. I was looking out the window, watching them come closer and closer, wondering how to escape.

Like most dreams, I would wake up before the 'encounter of the awful kind' took place. The nightmares always left me with a quaking body and a pounding heart. I dreaded going to bed at night. I could always expect the same horrific night hag bringing her phantasm cinema.

These abhorrent dreams had other recurring themes as well: being pursued by evil, losing things or pets, being abandoned. Feelings of abandonment had started in my childhood. I was about three years old when my mother divorced my father for adultery, and she remarried immediately. The new marriage was stormy, with frequent yelling and fighting. Their fighting frightened me. I would always go outside or hide, trying to be invisible.

I never formed a bonding relationship with my stepfather. I never crawled on his lap, never wanted him to hug me, and I never called him Daddy. Now I know why—I was afraid of him.

Unaccustomed to children, a high-strung wife, and a demanding job with long hours, my stepfather had little time or incentive to build a bonding relationship with his stepdaughter. There was no bridge between us. I was left stranded, without guidance or comfort.

Step-parenthood in the child's heart is never a given. It is earned. Many stepfathers have little interest in the new wife's children, and heartily wish that the woman had come unencumbered.[1]

As the years passed, Mother experienced numerous bouts of mental illness. She was in the mental hospital several times, receiving therapy and shock treatments, along with mind-numbing drugs. Riddled with guilt, Mother kept herself in bondage to hidden secrets that compounded her nervousness. Unable to cope, she floated through life without a meaningful focus.

In My Mother's House

*Hidden in my mother's house were many secret stories,
restless to be told, buried deep in shaky hearts,
entangled in the past, entombed far back in time.
Like clouds hanging overcast, a darkened veil descended,
leaving us to wonder about missing puzzle pieces.*

—L.R.S.

Since she slept the days away, I became the mother to my younger siblings, who were four and nine years younger than I. There was no aunt, grandparent, neighbor, or close friend to confide in. I was instructed never to tell Mother anything that might make her nervous, so I was left to sort out my own difficulties.

My birth father never addressed the issue of my trauma. Oblivious to my grief, he would just rant and rave about safety, politics, and football.

As I reached into the past, I realized how little I knew about my father. What led him into a promiscuous lifestyle? His checkered past held few clues. The family sailed from Lithuania to America when he was less than five years old. His father never set foot on American soil; he died en route. His stepfather committed suicide; his mother never remarried.

Father was a middle child, lost in the shuffle of six siblings. With no father figure and a mother overwhelmed with traumas, little Harold's childhood was dismal. After completing the eighth grade, he left Minneapolis and tramped his way to Phoenix, Arizona. He never returned to school.

My father was very handsome, looking somewhat like the silent screen star Rudolf Valentino. Like Valentino he, too, was a gifted dancer, which led him into the arms of many women. That was probably the beginning of his search for lasting love, only to have each new union end with a fraudulent substitute. He was married six times, incapable of nurturing a lasting relationship.

I saw my father frequently while growing up, but it was like visiting a stranger. Other than our biological connection, we seemed to have little in common. Our conversations were generally about nothing.

My unresolved father hunger continued most of my life. In Frederick Buechber's book *Godric,* he wrote, "The sadness was I'd lost a father I had never fully found. It's like a tune that ends before you've heard it out. Your whole life through you search to catch the strain, and seek the face you've lost in strangers' faces."[2]

Why, I wondered, couldn't I have a *normal* mother and father?

I wanted a mother who would make sandwiches, cookies and lemonade, pack it all in a basket and whisk my siblings and me away to the beach—to the zoo—anywhere. I wanted a mother who made shopping and lunch dates with me. I wanted a mother I could confide in. I wanted a mother I didn't have to nurture all the time—I wanted nurturing.

My mother took me to church. For that I will be *eternally* grateful.

I wanted a father that I could count on. One who was always there for me; one who said I could do anything I set my mind to; one who would help me pick out a prom dress, take pictures of us together. I wanted a father who stayed with my mother all of his life; a father I would see loving and adoring my mother; a father I could admire and respect.

My father took me to the movies once. He took me to the horse races once.

I wanted a mother and father who did things together. I wanted a mother and father who did things with their children. I wanted *my* father and mother together.

When I was young, I used to console myself by saying, "It's all right. Maybe a poor relationship with my parents is good. Maybe I won't feel the pain of their passing and grieve like most people do. Maybe I won't hurt."

How ironic; what I wanted most from my parents, I never fully gave my children.

I pretended to be a part of the family, but isolation deepened within. With broken patches of tranquility, I survived my childhood, though I never fully lived it. Lingering shadows of profound loneliness, anger, and sadness darkened my path to adulthood as I continued my search for "home."

A couple of months after the rape, my husband tried to console me by taking me on a short trip to Arizona. While there we took an underground tour of some caves. As soon as I stepped into the elevator, I sensed it was a mistake. The small room felt like being in an icebox. It groaned, shook, and creaked as it jerked its way down. Finally, it stopped and the door opened, exposing a cold, wet wall. There was barely enough room for two people to walk beside each other. The elevator door closed and began yanking and crawling its way back up. Looking around, I felt suffocated, like a mummy in a coffin.

"Get me out of here!" I shrieked.

It seemed like an eternity before the elevator returned. My husband and I quickly stepped in and he pushed the UP button. As it hauled us back to the surface, jarring from side to side, I buried my head on my husband's chest. I didn't look up until the elevator door opened.

My rape trauma had left me so emotionally shaken that everything appeared negative and frightening. Days slipped by. Fear was my shadow, my gun my escort; I carried it even when feeding the horses.

I felt spied on all the time. The rapist's house was in view of our home, even though a deep ravine separated us. How convenient—he could stalk me from the privacy of his own front yard!

Boulders of unremitting agony weighed me down, crushing any positive thoughts I might have had. I felt like a time bomb of rage, tears, and fear, ready to explode at the slightest provocation.

Many days I sat on the hillside, with my head buried in my lap, crying for hours. My husband would silently stroll past, but he rarely reached out to console me. I wondered what he was thinking. Did he think I should be getting better and getting on with my life? Perhaps he thought I was just a crybaby. Maybe he just felt helpless. I didn't know. I only knew I was losing control of my emotions.

With feelings of hopeless abandonment, I slept too much and cried relentlessly. I wanted to run away and hide—which I did, a short time later.

Abandoned

I looked around; no one was there.
My spirit longed to share my hurt with someone who cared.
The blackness that gripped my life was
almost more than I could bear.
I was slowly slipping away, sinking deep
into a bottomless pit.
Some heard me, but didn't listen.
Mother, lost in her own abysmal world.
Father lectured; others whispered.
"Help! Does anyone care?"
Indifferent to my tears, he silently passed me by.
Abandoned by those I loved the most,
no one heard my cries.

—L.R.S.

WHAT IT'S ALL ABOUT

"Only those who have lost reality and lived for years in the Land of Cruel, Inhuman Enlightenment, can truly taste the joy in living and prize the transcendent significance of being a part of humanity."

—Marguerite Schehayae

On the average, one woman is raped somewhere in the United States every minute of every day. One out of every four women born in this country will be raped at some point in her life. According to FBI statistics, in the United States alone, more than 100,000 women report being raped each year, and an estimated additional 400,000 to 900,000 are raped, but do not report the crime.[3]

Myths about rape enable us to maintain our belief that we live in a just world. They allow us to believe we can prevent future rapes. They keep women unequal to men, living under their control and in need of their protection from harm. They maintain the Adam and Eve tradition of our culture, in which man is believed to be the innocent victim of the evil temptress, woman.[4]

During a rape, sex is used as a weapon to intimidate, control, and humiliate the victim. If rape were simply sexually motivated, Las Vegas, which is surrounded by legalized prostitution, would not have one of the highest rape rates in the nation; however, according to police statistics, it does.[5] As a society we cannot afford to tolerate treating rape and the degradation of women as a game.

Fear: Loss of Safety

The most widespread fear that rape survivors experience is the fear of death. In surveys conducted, over half of all survivors did not expect to live through the rape. Rape is a crime of violence and aggression, not a crime of passion.

For rapists, sex is a weapon used to degrade women and cause them pain. All during a rape, the woman fears for her life.

In Nancy Vanable Raine's book *After Silence,* she writes, "The loss of the sense of safety is impossible to regain once you have lost it. The sense of safety is not like other senses ... smell, taste, sight. It has no companions that can compensate for its absence. It stands alone, beneath, like the foundation below ground that supports a building. When the sense of safety and bodily autonomy have been destroyed, all that it supports crumbles. Its loss changes the relation between self and the world."[6]

She adds, "The need to feel safe can become an addiction that cannot be satisfied by external measures, although it takes many years to discover this. There will never be enough locks, security cameras, dogs, or doormen to satisfy this craving. When the sense of safety is destroyed, the temptation to construct it outside the self is itself the source of more addictions. You can spend a fortune and still find yourself sitting alone in the dark, trembling. Precautions, no matter how elaborate and sound, remain on the surface, like Sargasso. No roots descend into the mysterious depths where the wreck truly lies."[7]

Post-Traumatic Stress Disorder

Studies have found that if you were raped in a so-called safe place, such as your home, Post-Traumatic Stress Disorder will be greater than if it occurred in a place you considered dangerous, such as walking alone down a street late at night. More women are raped in their own homes than any other single place.

A person's brain chemistry can be altered by emotional jolts and sudden shocks. Medical problems and old age can change it also. This alteration can be temporary, or once off balance it can remain off balance. If necessary treatment is not taken, the balance can get further out of kilter.

Shame

After rape, women experience a sense of shame and guilt. The feeling of shame is so intense that many never tell anyone what happened to them. Even in a psychotherapeutic setting, victims of rape often avoid talking about their traumas.

According to Michael Lewis, in his 1992 study *Shame: The Exposed Self,* an intense feeling of shame can cause memory loss. Shame silences because it encloses the entire self. Rape shame is hard to escape.

Shame is what the rapist, not the victim, should feel. Yet his shame is transferred to the victim, and her shame renders her mute.

"Aristotle describes shame as the feeling that involves things that are disgraceful to ourselves or to those we care for. Shame is fear of a public exhibition of wrongdoing, of being exposed in front of the group. He recognized this when he said, 'Shame is a mental picture of disgrace in which we shrink from the disgrace itself, and not from its consequences.'"[8]

Depression

Disturbances in a human being's neurotransmitter system occur when he or she has been subjected to severe stress, which can lead to depression. The strained biochemistry cannot perform its functions as it did before the traumatic event. Classic symptoms of the neurotransmitter system breaking down are hypersensitivity to others, irritability, anxiety, loss of the ability to experience peace, and loss of interest in life in general.

In his book *The Surprising Truth about Depression*, Herbert Wagemaker, M.D., declared, "Depression is difficult to describe. You might say depression is just a feeling. You might say it's like living inside a dark cloud—no light, no hope. Then again, you might liken depression to a state of paralysis. You can't think. You can't even move. You feel like you simply can't go on with your life.

These kinds of feelings are incomprehensible to those who have never suffered from depression. But to those who have, they are woven into the very fabric of their lives."[9]

Recovery

Courtenay Harding of the University of Colorado asked a number of trauma victims, "What really made the difference in your recovery?" The most common answer: people who told them they had a chance to get better. Knowing that others believed in them translated into hope. Without hope, death can establish a foothold. Hope fights fear and nurtures courage. It inspires vision, which is essential to beginning the work required to realize the unattainable.

"It isn't one person or incident or clinical intervention that is critical for change to occur. Instead, it's a complex process. One essential factor is keeping the spirit alive.

Connecting with others helps; receiving respect and warmth breaks through the isolation, and helps you feel worthwhile and alive." [10]

Everyone Has a Dark Side

Our dark side is the nature of sin into which we were born. What we do with our sin nature affects our way of life. Thomas

Moore, in his book *Care of the Soul,* wrote, "In studying the mythologies of the world, you always find evil characters in some sort of underworld; the same is true of the family. It always has its shadow, no matter how much we wish otherwise."[11]

> Mercy and truth are met together; righteousness and peace
> have kissed each other. Truth shall spring out of the earth;
> and righteousness shall look down from heaven.
> —Psalm 85:10-11 (KJV)

The Ladies' Tree

"I was captive to fear in my own body, subjected to mental torture, reliving the trauma over and over again in my mind."

—L.R.S.

Another clear, sunny day, I was driving by myself to Riverside for a court hearing. I told my husband I would be fine. Although I should have been feeling as nice as the weather, I wasn't. I felt cold and empty, like a marble statue. Down deep, I wanted someone to go with me, but I never asked; I didn't want to bother anyone. Self-pity, paying its price of aloneness, brought my self-esteem about as low as it could go.

As I approached the courthouse, I made a left turn and immediately stopped when I realized I had turned onto a one-way street, going the wrong way. As I started to back up, flashing red lights blinked in my rearview mirror. "Oh, no," I muttered.

Already nervous about the hearing, I burst into tears. I tried to explain where I was going and why.

The officer's attitude was, "So what?" He just stood there, matter-of-fact, stone-faced, and proceeded to write a ticket, all the while preaching a little sermon about me being a nitwitted woman for not paying attention. I hadn't even arrived at the courthouse and already felt defeated.

I don't remember much of the rest of the day. I only recall being on the witness stand, answering questions that were fired at me, and feeling like the criminal instead of the victim. The interrogation was painful, accusing, and demeaning. It left me shaken and weary.

After the trial, the rapist was convicted and sentenced to the Atascadero State Prison for the insane. The threatening phone calls stopped; my apprehension did not.

In the book *Joan of Arc: In Her Own Words,* compiled and translated by Willard Trask, Joan tells a story from her girlhood.

"Not far from Domremy there is a tree called the Ladies' Tree, and others called it Faries' Tree, and near it there is a fountain. And I heard that those who are sick with fever drink at the fountain or fetch water from it to be made well. I have heard, too, that the sick, when they can get up, go walking under the tree. It is a great tree, a beech. Sometimes I walked there with other girls and made garlands under the tree. I have often heard it said by old people that the faries met there. I never saw any faries under the tree. I have seen girls hang wreaths on the branches.

"There is a wood in Domremy, called the Polled Wood; you can see it from my father's door. When I was on my journey to my King, I was asked by some if there was a wood in my country called the Polled Wood, for it had been prophesied that a maid would come from near that wood to do wonderful things. But I said, I had no faith in that."[1]

How desperately I wanted to find the "Ladies' Tree." I was mentally ill and wanted immediate healing. I wanted to walk under the beautiful beech tree with its graceful branches and hang garlands and daisy chains of restoration. I wanted to walk under the Farie Tree, to sing and dance with joy and be restored to the woman I was before that season of darkness. I wanted to drink from the fountain of wellness and quench my thirst for peace.

I also wanted to be the Maid from the Polled Wood, coming to do wonderful things. But like Joan of Arc, I too said I had no faith in that. My faith was shattered. Not in God, but in mankind. Whom could I trust? To whom could I turn? Who cared? I was in a fight for survival all by myself, or so I thought. The future held the healing; time and God had much to teach me—I would have to wait. The race to wellness proceeded at a snail's pace.

Mental illness, like the falling leaves . . . the quiet death no one sees.[2]

WHAT IT'S ALL ABOUT

"Man is the only animal who causes pain to others with no other object than wanting to do so."
—Schopenhauer, On Ethics, Paralipomena, 1851

Secondary Wounding: Recovery

It's important to the healing process to have people come alongside you. Unfortunately, sometimes people do more harm than good. Secondary wounding occurs when people who do not understand your situation are unintentionally cruel.

Family, friends, and professionals are often cruel also. They can make you feel stupid or ashamed of having been raped. They wonder about your reactions to the event and question why you would seek help. People who have never been trau-matized have difficulty understanding victims and tend to lack patience with them. The very ones we turn to for emotional support are sometimes the ones who let us down.

Linda E. Ledray, in her book *Recovering from Rape*, writes, "We all have only a certain amount of energy available for deal-ing with stressful events in our lives. Dealing with rape uses up a lot of that energy, so we don't have much left over."

She adds, "The experience of having your case go to court is another stress for you and for all your friends and family. Years of studies and research in all types of crises, including rape, show that next to your own resilience, the key factor in your recovery is support from family and friends. This is a time of turmoil. You are afraid you'll never recover, but you will."[3]

More Memories

The dark subconscious is a shadow world, and one compo-nent of this world is memory. More often than they would like, memories remind people of things in their lives they cannot control—things they have repressed or just plain prefer to forget. Memory is pain. Jung called this invasion the shadow at its worst.[4]

Every day, memories are stored in our subconscious minds. Later, we don't even remember they exist. Taine puts it this way: "In the struggle of life in which all our images are con-stantly engaged, the one furnished with the most force treads down its adversaries."

The human brain houses two types of minds: a feeling mind and a thinking mind. It uses a special method to make emo-tional memories come into focus with accurate potency. That same neurochemical system that alerts the body to react to life-threatening emergencies by fighting or fleeing also recalls our traumas with vividness. It demands that we react today in the same way we did to the trauma that occurred long ago. Our thoughts, emotions, and reactions respond to current events that are perhaps only vaguely similar, but close enough to alarm us. Traumatic memories sometimes trigger a warning that the dread moment is about to happen again. These hair-trigger moments hallmark emotional trauma of all kinds.

Post-Traumatic Stress Disorder leaves a person reacting to life's routine moments as if they were life threatening. A single instance of terror can alter the chemistry of the brain; the more indelible and horrifying the event, the more indelible the memory.

George Johnson, in his book *In the Palaces of Memory*, writes, "The experience of reading or conversing causes physical changes in your brain. In a matter of seconds new circuits are formed, memories that can change forever the way you think about the world. Memory leaves its mark so that we are able to carry around the past inside our heads. Every time you walk away from an encounter, your brain has been altered, sometimes permanently.

"The obvious but disturbing truth is that people can impose these changes against your will. Someone can say something— an insult, a humiliation; it lives with you as long as you live. The memory is physically lodged inside you like a shard of glass healed inside a wound. Experience is transformed into memories. Neuron by neuron, we snap together mental structures, constantly evolving palaces of memory that we carry with us until we die. Even as memories are being laid down, the brain is consolidating, and rearranging. Remembering is like being in a trance. Raw experience has been converted into a few set pieces. And it is the set pieces that are remembered."[5]

Recorded in your brain is a mental tape you cannot erase. The slightest thing can trigger an instant visual replay, causing you to re-experience the trauma you want to forget.

A sudden noise, murky shadows, a ringing phone at an unexpected hour, or a knock at the door would push the REPLAY button of my memories, leaving me hostage to daytime nightmares.

Biblical Insight

"The God of biblical faith is a God who started history in the first place. As I understand it, to say that God is mightily present even in such private events as this does not mean that He makes events happen which move us in certain directions like chessmen. Instead, events happen under their own steam as random as rain. This means that God is present in them, not as their cause, but as the one who, even in the hardest and most hair-raising of them, offers the possibility of that new life and healing . . ."[6]

"Sin in early Christian times (the accounts in Genesis of the creation of human beings and of their expulsion from the Garden of Eden), has been used to explain and justify the subordination of woman to man, and to fix responsibility for humanity's fallen state firmly on the shoulders of woman. Eve came to be seen as responsible for what Christian theology deems the original sin, the transgression that would stain all future generations."[7]

"There is the *perception* (italics mine), hardly open to question, that the Hebrew Bible and the New Testament deal with women harshly, negatively, and unfairly in many spheres, the need to understand why they do; the conviction, among some women, that alternative past awaits recovery. Among certain feminist scholars there is a belief, too, that recovering the past could help change the present."[8]

God did not intend for humanity to oppress itself. He created man and woman, and said everything was good. Later Satan, the purveyor of deceit, roared in. And the rest is history.

Divorce: A Side Effect of Rape

In Jim Conway's book *Adult Children of Divorce*, he writes, "When parents divorce, their children lose home, security, past history, and the hope of a positive future. Children feel abandoned as the home disintegrates."[9]

Wallerstein, Lewis and Blakeslee say, "For children, divorce is a watershed that permanently alters their lives. The world is newly perceived as a far less reliable, more dangerous place because the closest relationships in their lives can no longer be expected to hold firm. More than anything else, this new anxiety represents the *end of childhood.* Children of divorce need more time to grow up because they have to accomplish more; they must simultaneously let go of the past and create mental models for where they are headed, carving their own way. Those who succeed deserve gold medals for integrity and perseverance. Having rejected their parents as role models, they have to invent who they want to be and what they want to achieve in adult life. This is far and beyond what most adolescents are expected to achieve."[10]

It is very common for couples to divorce after the rape of a spouse. Rape bears down hard on the strength of the links that hold a marriage together. But divorce is a long, painful path that seems to never end. Pursued by memory and attachment (children), along with unrelenting guilt, the wounds continue to fester.

CHAPTER 3

Nutcracker Suite

"A man who is of 'sound mind' is one who keeps the inner madman under lock and key."
—Valery, Mauvaises Pensees at Autres, 1942

Corona, California,1969: Fall. My rape trauma tore at the seams of my marriage, shredding it to pieces. Our relationship wasn't smooth before the rape, and I was a tyrant after it. I was on edge, defensive, and impatient. I put up walls of resistance. I felt angry, and nobody seemed to care. In general, I was a mess; my emotions were out of control. My depression had smothered any fire left in our marriage.

As a child I remember telling myself I would never get a divorce. I considered it hideous, like a death in the family. Forgetting my childhood vow, I filed for divorce.

I was ashamed of my divorce. I avoided my church, my long-time friends, and my family. I was miserable; the children, heart-broken.

I moved out of the house with the girls, got a job in a business office, and tried to start a new life. During that time,

I raged. I was promiscuous, drank, and acted rude. My mouth was a wide-open grave with a poison tongue emitting venomous fumes of contempt.

My new life left me immobile, empty. I couldn't concentrate on anything and often burst into tears over nothing. Depression consumed me.

Seductive deception crouched at my door with mocking voices chanting, "Suicide!" I had reached the end of the tracks, like being on a train to nowhere. I wanted to disconnect from the world, if not through death then at least into a safe hiding place. I chose to try the hiding place first.

I believe my rape, this cruel invasion of my security, was what triggered my mental breakdown. My body was put in an "alarm reaction state" in order to cope with my attack, and thus produced high levels of hormones. Compounding this with a family history of chemical imbalance, my emotional and reasoning power slid downhill, destined to collapse.

I wasn't insane, but my mental health was unstable. I couldn't cope in my present state of mind; I knew I needed help. I decided to check out a mental hospital in Pomona, California—which I affectionately called the Nutcracker Suite—intending to stay a short while.

It felt strange standing there at the reception counter, filling out patient admittance forms on myself. I'd watched this scene acted out with my mother many times. But the play was different now. This time I was the main character.

I gazed around the lobby, and my eyes fell on the locked No Admittance door. I knew once I passed through that door, I might not exit for some time. But I didn't care. I wanted solitude, to be left alone. I didn't want to talk to anyone.

A nurse with jangling keys and shuffling feet ushered me through that ominous door. I carried nothing but a small overnight bag.

Entering my modest room, I gazed around. Compact night-stands sat beside twin beds with a privacy curtain separating them. A dark cavity of a window yawned on the opposite wall.

My days were scheduled routines. Early breakfast, then go to the nurse's station for my ration of pills, some of which left me in a zombie stupor. Free time, lunch, more pills, afternoon group therapy. More free time, more pills, and then dinner. Day in and day out, it was always the same.

Group therapy was held in a room with a long table surrounded by chairs. The counselor and his assistant sat at each end of the table with their notebooks, ready to probe information from us. I was always defensive, sarcastic, and stubborn, leaving each meeting as empty as when I went in.

There was a common room where patients could watch television, but I never did. I didn't enjoy television, couldn't concentrate, and didn't want to be with other people. I preferred to go out every day and soak in the warm sun, breathe the fresh air, and admire the garden. That was probably the most therapeutic session I received. I thought about nothing as I closed my eyes and listened to the sounds of passing traffic, birds singing, the voices of people walking by on the sidewalk, the drone of an overhead airplane, a siren in the distance, and occasionally a barking dog.

I missed my children and the dogs. The girls were staying with my sister in Oregon, and the dogs were with my ex-husband. While I was growing up, I'd clung to my pets as one would to a life raft in churning waters. I loved them, and they loved me—unconditionally.

The days passed into weeks, and the weeks into months. I felt as if I were in a holding pattern—like a jet circling the runway waiting for clearance to land. I could not stay forever in my Nutcracker Suite, nor did I want to. But I needed to keep circling the runway while I gathered the fragments of my life. After I pieced them together, then I could touch down to reality.

Would I ever be well again? Had I ever been well? What was it like to feel normal? I didn't know.

I received few phone calls, and only two visitors. Like putrid water, I was beginning to stagnate, lying dormant in my self-pity. I felt suspended in time.

Then one day I knew it was time to leave the security of my cocoon, spread my wings, and fly. Propelled by some inner drive, I stepped out into the real world, ready to face my solo flight. I didn't know where my valor or tenacity was going to come from, but God did. Walking out of the hospital through the same lobby I'd entered just a few months before made my Nutcracker Suite experience feel like just a dream.

Had I really recovered from my traumas and pain in the hospital? Unfortunately, no. My hardened heart and negative attitude wouldn't let me budge one bit toward recovery. I'd spent my time in seclusion alone, which had allowed me to think—but I hadn't bothered doing any thinking about God. I didn't want Him interfering with the justification for my anger, resentment, and bitterness.

My frame of mind did not allow me to consider that God could love me, much less that He could restore me. I felt like a complete failure, and I figured God viewed me the same way. My faith in His love for me was weak, nearly nonexistent. I didn't realize His love for me was strong and everlasting.

A recurring evil dream haunted me. I was being chased by people and creatures. I sought shelter in a tall building, but the people and creatures tried to break into the building. I put numerous padlocks on the doors and windows. I wanted to go to the restroom, but there wasn't any privacy there. They peeped in through tiny openings, looking for a way in. I wanted to escape in my car, but there was a creature in it.

When awake, I interpreted this dream as the rapist continuing his quest, trying to destroy me through my mind. No matter what I tried to do to force him away, he still intruded through the minute pockets of my soul. Malevolence marched, wounding me.

But my rapist hadn't returned after that night. I was now at war with another enemy—Satan.

O little bird, floating free in the air,
thou hit the glass, hurling thee to the ground.
Thou mate close upon, taking wing, lifted thee,
and like a chariot in the sky, soared off
to lay thee at rest and mourn thy loss.

—L.R.S.

For a while, I lived in a two-story house with floor-to-ceiling windows. One morning, as I was looking outside, a small bird flew into the window, then dropped to the ground, either unconscious or dead. Within a split second, another bird flew to the ground, picked it up, and carried it away. The first bird had been dealt a harmful blow, and its mate could not bear to leave it. The tenderness of that moment left a lasting impression with me. If only humans were as compassionate.

I felt like that little bird after my rape. I had been floating free when something threw me into the window of fear and pain, hurling me to the ground. It wasn't my mate that rescued me; it was my heavenly Father. He tenderly lifted me up and carried me on His wings of love.

II Corinthians 4:7-8 says we are jars of clay to be treasured. We may feel pressed, persecuted, and struck down; however, we are not destroyed or abandoned by Him. I decided to trust Him for my destination and restoration.

I moved to Oregon in 1975 and remarried. The following years held trials and errors, detours, potholes and more lessons to be learned. As I bounced along, I didn't know a divine appointment with God was waiting ahead. I was to receive a promise from Him—a promise that would come to pass and change me forever. This time, for my good.

WHAT IT'S ALL ABOUT

Sometime before morning, brave new wings took flight. Below stood madness mocking as she threw away the night.[1]

Soul Murder

"The soul of mankind, with all its tremendous faculties . . . moves in silence, judgment, without any racket, lifting its scales; memory, without any noise, bringing down all its treasurer's conscience, taking its judgment seat without any excitement; the understanding and the will all doing their work. Velocity, majesty, might; but silence . . . silence. You listen at the door of your heart. You can hear no sound. The soul is all quiet. It is so delicate an instrument that no human hand can touch it. You may break a bone, and with splinters and bandages the surgeon sets it; the eye becomes inflamed, the apothecary's wash cools it; but a soul off the track, unbalanced, no human power can readjust it."[2]

In Strinberg's 1887 article "Soul Murder," Ibsen Rosmersholm said, "Soul murder is defined as taking away a person's reason for living. The capacity to destroy a soul hinges entirely on having another human be in one's power.

"When one person absorbs the life of another, he commits soul murder. Soul or psychic murder involves trauma *imposed* from the world outside the mind that is so overwhelming that the mental apparatus is flooded with feeling. The same overstimulated state can result as a reaction to a great deprivation. The terrifying too-muchness requires massive and mind-distorting defensive operations to continue to think, feel and live."[3]

Soul murder is as old as human history, as ageless as the abuse of the helpless by the powerful in any group . . . which means as old as the family.[4] I prefer to call soul murder *soul trauma,* as the soul never really dies.

Because the soul never dies, it belongs to either Satan or God. No one can steal it except the devil; but only with permission.

I knew my damaged soul belonged to God and that He could restore it. He was just waiting for my invitation.

Depression

Herbert Wagemaker, M.D., says in his book *The Surprising Truth about Depression,* "Some Christians sometimes have suicidal thoughts. When you are in the midst of depression, you don't have control of such thoughts. This is also a part of depression, especially severe depression. What you do have control over is whether or not you seek out treatment, and you should do so as soon as possible."[5]

Stress

When traumatic crises hit, victims are overwhelmed by a state of emotional instability, a sort of temporary insanity characterized by intense fear and often painful physical symptoms. The usual coping mechanisms are inadequate. New ways of dealing with this period of dangerous stress must be found. Victims' perceptions of reality become totally distorted, and their lives become a whirlwind of confusion, fear, and depression.[6]

If the victims learn new problem-solving techniques, face the crises head-on, and resolve any issues that arise, they will grow. However, if the victims let their grief and pain bury them, they will drown in their suffering and ultimately regress into emotional basket cases. The victims are under the crushing weight of severe emotional pain and deep psychological wounds. The wounds are prone to reopening time and time again.[7]

Psychic Pain

Nancy Venable claimed in her book *After Silence*, "New studies into the destructive path that overwhelming experiences cut through the neural pathways of the brain suggest that getting over it is nothing short of miraculous. We are learning that the experience of living can never be the same after an overwhelming experience because the brain that experiences that life may not be the same brain."[8]

Broken Vessel

My heart ached so long, my soul I thought was dead.
I hid inside myself, a broken vessel, weeping bitter tears.
But You, O Holy One, never left my side.
You healed my heart, restored my soul
Through the passing years.

—L.R.S.

Forget the former things; do not dwell on the past. See, I am doing a new thing! Now it springs up; do you not perceive it?

—Isaiah 43:18-19

CHAPTER 4

His Name Is Crackers

"He was all that, Satan, in the form of the rapist; a damnable force continuing to tamper with the biological wiring of my mind, causing it to malfunction."

—L.R.S.

Another dream came to me at this time. Secret chambers of my mind replayed my past in vivid color. I traveled back in time to my birthplace—Phoenix, Arizona—to experience childhood once again.

I wandered around town, seeking out familiar places. I passed tall buildings, Indians on street corners pitching their wares, and store vendors selling cheap goods from Mexico. A few palm trees and cacti offered feeble shade as the blistering sun scorched the dusty ground.

The wonderful smells of the old five-and-dime store drew me in. Cheap perfumes, cosmetics, baby powder, soda fountain ice cream—vanilla, of course—hot dogs, and buttered popcorn.

The sights were just as enticing: tacky trinkets, cheesy clothing, comic books, toys, and gaudy jewelry. I wanted to be there again in real life, as a little girl tasting awe and wonder anew, soaking in the simpleness of that era.

As I walked the streets, a little girl appeared at my side. I told her I would show her the tavern my father owned when I was young. The tavern in my dream was a sidewalk bar where patrons sat on high stools and placed their orders. My father stood behind the counter, washing and drying glasses.

Because we were invisible, he couldn't see us. I felt sad; I wanted to talk to him, ask questions about his early life, and tell him I was sorry we didn't have a closer relationship. When he was alive, I knew he was never at peace; a man unfulfilled, seeking happiness in all the wrong places—leaving God out of his life.

My young friend and I went to the old movie theater, where vintage posters displayed movies of the '40s, featuring stars such as Rita Hayworth, Susan Hayword, Ava Gardner, Cornel Wilde, and Clark Gable.

Then the little girl disappeared, as suddenly as she had appeared.

Leaving the downtown area, I drifted toward the back streets. There, I came upon a man with a dark complexion and a head of black, bushy hair. He was robbing a bank, pointing his gun at a crowd of people and saying he was going to kill a relative.

I heard the police called him Crackers. They said he was a gangster. The crowd cowered in fear, waiting for the police to capture him.

Finally, the rapist had a name in my mind—Crackers. I learned the word is British slang for "insane." The name fit him perfectly; he went to a prison for the insane.

This was one of many horrific dreams that haunted me for years. While I loved God, I didn't understand Him or His ways. Satan, hearing negative words tumble from my mouth, used my traumas as a springboard for more evil. He launched an attack of lies about God and mankind with all the fiery darts he possessed. And it worked—for a season.

The enemy got inside the gates, took prisoners
of loving memories, made casualties of dreams.[1]

Dark Dream

I ran in the night down dark roads,
only to see you close behind.
I hid, hoping you wouldn't find me.
Then you were there.
I could almost feel your breath.
I ran again in the black side of day,
praying never to be caught.
Maybe if I killed you, you couldn't return,
and I wouldn't have to run.

—L.R.S.

WHAT IT'S ALL ABOUT

Memories are sometimes the uninvited guests whom we must forgive for intruding.[2]

Memories

When a woman has been sexually assaulted, she is given a life sentence of memories that can surface at any time. These traumatic memories are often stored deep in the subconscious mind. When they return, they may not arise as a coherent story, but rather as a fragment of a story.

Psychic pain is the result of traumatic memories we cannot get rid of. To experience a traumatic event is enough to engrave the picture in one's mind instantly, permanently storing the negative image. When under extreme stress, our brains produce noradrenaline, releasing it into our bloodstream, expanding our awareness. Flashbulbs go off, capturing the adrenaline-filled trauma in our minds, leaving us with vivid mental photos of pain.

Social Crisis

Rape is a social crisis. One of the most important things you can do for the survivor is to help her rebuild her internal sense of security. When a woman has been assaulted in her home, her sanctuary can become a constant reminder of that which she wishes to forget. Safety feels foreign, and fear follows relentlessly. Some women cannot move due to financial reasons, and others may not want to.

> Blessed is she who has believed that what the Lord had said to her will be accomplished!
>
> —Luke 1:45

CHAPTER 5

The Promise

"My 'happy pill' gathered up all my shaky emotions, put them in a calm, loving basket, and politely told them to hush up."

—L.R.S.

Bend, Oregon, 1995: Summer. Half asleep, I stumbled into the living room and plopped on the sofa. A heavy shroud—depression—surrounded me, pressing in, trying to crush life from me. It followed me constantly. Once again, my emotions were like leaves in a whirlwind, tossed and scattered every which way. I knew I had to get control of them.

I cried a lot, was edgy, and just wanted to be left alone. I might as well have been in another room when conversing with others. I could not grasp their words. Their voices were strange, colorless. I would look into their faces, hear the drone of their words, but was unable to comprehend. Intruding thoughts of escaping their presence flooded my mind. I struggled to repress them, but they absorbed me. I kept thinking, *I've got to get out of here!*

The chemical imbalance in my brain was racing at a dangerous speed. I needed more help than I could give myself. I needed a doctor—again.

God, I have tried so hard. I have nothing left to give. Help me!

I stared out the window, past the deck, the lawn, and the juniper trees. I gazed transfixed upon the pond; it was beautiful. A lone goose paddled through the morning mist that floated above the still water. Around three o'clock, a breeze would sail in, causing little waves to ripple and lap at the grassy bank. I sat in silence, listening for God to respond to my plea.

Then, like a ticker tape flashing through my mind, a thought came: *I will bring peace to your life like the calm on the morning pond.*

I sat there dumbfounded, not quite believing what I had heard.

The thought came again: *I will bring peace to your life like the calm on the morning pond.*

I wasn't imagining it; it was loud and clear in my head. God had spoken.

I dragged myself to the edge of the sofa and leaned forward. *You will? Okay, I can wait another day—what have I got to lose—only my life.* I didn't know how God was going to bring peace into my life, but I knew if He said He would, He would. He had the perfect plan for my future—if I didn't get in His way. Controlling my emotions and waiting patiently would be another test of fire. I sighed, lay down, and fell asleep.

As the days passed, some were wrinkled, and some were smooth. I accepted the smooth ones with gratitude and tried not to question the wrinkled ones.

My doctor prescribed an anti-depressant to correct the chemical imbalance and, theoretically, cure my depression. I was desperate and willing to try anything for peace.

A week went by, and I wasn't depressed. As a matter of fact, I felt wonderful.

Amazing! And all it took was a little pill.

This must be what it's like to feel normal. I'm not crazy. Thank You, God!

At first, I called my anti-depressant my "crazy pill," and then later, I decided I should call it my "happy pill."

More days passed. Summer moved along. I was finally beginning to enjoy life. I wasn't depressed, and I wasn't out of control, but I still felt fearful occasionally, especially at night.

After my rape, I never slept in bed when my husband was out of town, always on the sofa. I kept a gun, car keys, and a flashlight beside me, ready to make a quick getaway.

There were times I would sleep on the floor by the front door. I once fled with my dogs to a motel to escape unbearable fear that washed over me. I was captive to fear in my body, subjected to mental torture, reliving the trauma over and over again in my mind.

One morning at the end of a church service, the visiting pastor called my husband and me to the front of the congregation. Having never met us before, he asked a few questions. He announced that we would be celebrating something special in six months, then pointed his finger at me and said, "You are not to be afraid of the night anymore."

I was stunned. Only God knew the depth of my debilitating nighttime fears. Surely God was telling me, through this prophetic word, that I was to be set free, once and for all. God's grace would make a way of escape for me.

Still, I questioned myself. I wondered if I would ever be able to sleep in my own bed without my husband beside me to make me feel safe.

My test of fire came all too soon. A couple of days after receiving that prophecy, my husband left on a business trip.

As bedtime drew near, a thought flashed in my mind: *You can go to bed now.* Those words played around in my head as the evening wore on and I wore out.

Finally I said, "God, will You be mad at me if I don't sleep in my bed tonight? I want to, and I know Your word is true. But would it be okay if I tried tomorrow night?" I felt terrible for my cowardliness and lack of faith. Yet I also felt comforted and assured as I settled onto the couch for the night.

I kept my word the following night. After much procrastination, I crawled into bed. It felt strange, alone in the ominous, silent dark.

I drew a deep breath. "Okay, God, here I am. I'm doing my part—now You do Yours. Help me not to be afraid."

I closed my eyes, said my prayers, and tried to relax. I glanced at my Rottweiler sleeping soundly at the foot of my bed and felt some measure of comfort. Was that cheating?

I slept through the night.

My original fear was real and justified when the attacker was trying to break into our home, while he was raping me, and even for a period of time after the event. But worry is not true fear. Worry is *anticipating* that something bad might happen. Worry is Satan's lies translated into fear.

I will lie down and sleep in peace, for You alone, O Lord, make me dwell in safety.

—Psalm 4:8

Escape

*I ran as fast as I could, trying to escape the
black clouds engulfing my mind,
Pressing in with no relief, crushing my heart,
leaving me sad and full of despair.
Running, always running, all day and on into the night . . .
Trying to ignore my daunting spirit,
I was slowly dying inside.
With abandoned hope, I poured out my soul
to the heavenly Father above.
His breath of life flowed in me, loosened the bonds,
and set me free.*

—L.R.S.

WHAT IT'S ALL ABOUT

"That which does not kill makes us stronger . . . at least eventually."

—Anne Elizabeth

The Spoils of Victory

In this world, women cannot win the unmitigated war of rape. The climate of violence leaves them afraid of the predator who walks the streets looking very average, like your favorite uncle, mailman, school teacher, or preacher. Educated to believe that men are caring and will protect women, they find that the men they trust can violate them.

Rape is considered a criminal act under the international rules of war and is punishable by death or imprisonment. Yet newspapers continually alert us to ethnic cleansings where thousands of women and young girls have been raped and plundered in the name of war. Men felt it was their right—"All's fair in love and war." The sickness of warfare feeds on itself. Some soldiers must prove their superiority to a woman, to themselves, and to other men. In the name of victory and the power of the gun, men see themselves given a license to rape.

The Bible, in Deuteronomy 20:14, tells us, "As for the women . . . you may take as plunder for yourself." Ancient Greeks considered captured women as legitimate booty.

I will give you a new heart and put a new spirit in you; I will remove from you your heart of stone and give you a heart of flesh.

—Ezekiel 36:26

CHAPTER 6

The Loud, Silent Year

"Like the ancient serpent, we slither back through the time tunnel and pick up where Adam and Eve left off."

—L.R.S.

I told myself, "Someday, I'm going to write a book about my experiences." Over the years, I took writing classes, went to writer's seminars and joined a critique group. I had written and published poems and articles, but nothing as daunting as a full-length book.

In 1996 I became an advocate with the Washington County Sexual Assault Resource Center. I co-facilitated classes for women in recovery from rape. While the program was enlightening, it frustrated me that the spiritual needs of the women were unmet. I decided I wanted to offer women a class where such needs could be met. Thus began inquisition for this book.

After months of research, I started my first chapter. It never went beyond one sentence. It was scary to relive every traumatic moment sentence-by-sentence. I put it aside and tried again the next day. I was like a cold car engine, sputtering a few words at a time. That went on for days. Then one morning my fear seemed to disappear. The words began to flow.

As I wrote, I thought only of negative cause and effects. But I knew somehow, somewhere, there had to be a positive side. As I continued to write, little by little, affirmative images emerged.

After completing about three-fourths of the manuscript, my writing came to an abrupt halt—again. I couldn't understand what was happening—or should I say, not happening. I tried to write, but the words simply wouldn't come. I didn't seem to have any more to say. The manuscript sat on a shelf for more than a year, collecting dust.

During that time of waiting, I yielded myself to God, trusting more words would come, or they wouldn't. I believed whatever took place would be His will; the writing would be left as is, or the story completed.

When the psyche has been deeply wounded, the evil one marches in and starts a spiritual battle. He tries to smash our spiritual strength, leaving us weak, defiant, and defensive, especially with God. This defiant, prideful contempt locks us into suffering and continues a pact with the devil. Beneath a veneer of contentment may be hidden despair, pounding to get out, but locked in our hearts due to prideful stubbornness. Broken dreams and failed beginnings may appear to defeat us. With Christ, they can never destroy us; however, they can reveal who we are.

I could not continue to hang on to past wounds as an excuse to justify my anger, rage, and bitterness. How could holding on serve a positive purpose? I needed to remember the past in a different way.

"Forgiving is agreeing to live with the consequences of someone else's sin."[1]

The God of mercy pierced my spirit, making me a poster child for His grace. I never exhausted Him of His love and patience for me. The spotlight of my rebellious attitude gave way to a teachable attitude, allowing me to hear Him speak in what I thought was a silent year. It became probably one of the most profound years of my life. God spoke, and I listened—for a change.

Healing the present meant I had to embrace the past with an open heart. I had to trust God. *I needed to forgive.* I needed to push aside disappointments and sorrow for the healing path to begin. This path would lead me to discover myself, the way God intended.

Neil Anderson, Terry Zuehlke, and Julianne Zuehlke say, in their book *Christ-Centered Therapy*, "Traumatic experiences contribute to the formation of the attitude. They are buried deep in our minds and they are what keep people in bondage to the past, not the traumatic experience itself."[2] The difference is our *perception*. We cannot undo the reality of events that have taken place in our lives. But with God's power, we can change the effect those events have on us in the present.

The acceptance of our wounded psyche can lead us to grace, forgiveness, love, and compassion. Lewis B. Smedes said in his book *Forgive & Forget*, "Forgiving does not reduce evil. Forgiving great evil does not shave a millimeter from its monstrous size. When we forgive evil we do not excuse it, we do not tolerate it, and we do not smother it. We look evil full in the face, call it what it is, let its horror shock, stun and enrage us, and only then do we forgive it. If we say that monsters are beyond forgiving, we give them a power they should never have. They are given power to keep their evil alive in the hearts of those who suffered most."[3]

He further states, "Forgiveness is God's invention for coming to terms with a world in which, despite their best intentions, people are unfair to each other and hurt each other deeply. He began by forgiving us. And He invites us all to forgive each other."[4]

Forgiveness is a matter of the heart. And forgiving is necessary for our souls to rest and be free of strongholds.

We all have things that have happened in our lives that we need to forgive someone for. And it is easier to forgive someone who has merely hurt your feelings than someone who has physically assaulted you. However, we must all arrive at the decision to forgive in our own time.

> "Forgiving is love's revolution against life's unfairness. When we forgive, we ignore the normal laws that strap us to the natural law of getting even and by the alchemy of love, we release ourselves from our own painful past."
> —Lewis B. Smedes

Forgiving is not excusing or condoning. It's letting go of strongholds that are keeping you in bondage. Forgiveness is not for God; it's for you, to be set free and feel the peace that surpasses all understanding, the kind only God can give. Until we forgive, we cannot escape the strongholds of pain.

Smedes said, "Remember, you cannot erase the past, you can only heal the pain it has left behind. When you are wronged, that wrong becomes an indestructible reality of your life. When you forgive, you heal your hate for the person who created that reality. But you do not change the facts. And you do not undo all of their consequences. The dead stay dead; the wounded are often crippled still. The reality of evil and its damage to human beings is not magically undone and it can still make us very mad."[5]

Don't confuse forgiveness with forgetting; they are not the same. Forgiveness begins with a decision, even if we don't feel like it. We do it because it will bring much-needed healing.

Debbie Morris, in her book *Forgiving the Dead Man Walking,* writes, "Much if not most of the time, our reluctance to forgive is based on the false assumption that forgiving means giving in or giving up something valuable. We think it might mean granting the other person some reward he or she doesn't deserve. Or completely discounting the wrong committed—as if it never happened. That's not how forgiveness works." She goes on to say, "By forgiving Robert Willie, I in no way absolved him of his responsibility for what he did to me. So forgiveness isn't giving him anything he doesn't deserve; he gains nothing from it." She concludes by saying, "Justice didn't do a thing to heal me. Forgiveness did."[6]

Hardened hearts, pride, anger, and revenge block the path to forgiveness. God's original plan for humankind didn't include injustice, but we experience it because of sin.

We can't escape it. God can counter our unwillingness to forgive by overwhelming us with truth, which is that we cannot forgive at the human level, with the intellect.

Consequences are what usually change our behavior. It is dangerous to believe we will never suffer the consequences of a hardened heart. The ugly consequences of my behavior led me to positive changes.

We can rise from suffering to victory when we realize that sorrow can be a necessary path for us to mature. We cannot always avoid tragedy and despair, nor should we, as they become tests of fire. We can emerge stronger, more confident individuals, or we can give in to our sin nature and accept defeat. If we choose the latter, our past is destined to be our future.

Our defense mechanism dates back to the Garden of Eden. Adam blamed Eve, and even God for giving her to him, and Eve blamed the serpent. That was probably the beginning of the blame game. We, too, are like Adam and Eve, blaming others for our sins and mistakes.

In Liberty Savard's book *Shattering Your Strongholds*, she says, "Something traumatic happens in my life which is a *fact* which leads me to develop a *wrong* pattern of thinking—which helps me *justify* a wrong behavior which causes me to erect strongholds to protect my right to do so, which perpetuates my pain by keeping the trauma locked in and God locked out."[7]

My traumas are a fact. Lies from Satan led me to develop wrong patterns of thinking about this fact, one of which was contempt. My wrong thinking led me to justify wrong behavior: a bad attitude, which produced rebellious actions, which made me think I had a right to do as I pleased even if it meant hurting others. This kept my pain inside and God out.

My mental instability was fertile ground for seeds of lies from Satan. He tried to steal my hope for the future by reminding me of lost dreams, failures, betrayals, and traumas. Early unwanted sexual encounters with men influenced my perception of them. My hostile, suspicious attitude clothed me in steel armor of distrust and unforgiveness. The armor had to be shattered in order for healing to come.

I was not about to thank the rapist or others who had turned my world upside down, but because of them, it caused me to look deep inside myself. I had been licking my wounds for years, and now it was time to face the truth and be set free. Because of God's grace, my series of unfortunate events and negative reactions did not destroy me. Instead, they eventually led to repentance, redemption, and God's calling on my life.

Weary from a sorrowful heart, I relented and repented. "Repented of what?" you may ask. "You were the one assaulted and wounded." True, but I had hardened my heart, allowing God in only as I felt like it. I had not yielded to a teachable spirit or a forgiving heart. That was rebellion toward God, and that was what I needed to repent of.

To go beyond tolerable recovery, one must learn to *deal* with disappointments, sorrow and trauma, not just *cope* with them. Here's the difference: *Coping* is like having a snake in your backyard and figuring out how to avoid it. Dealing with the snake is to remove it so you won't have to dodge it anymore.

Perhaps you have coped all your life with the past, bravely brushing it off by saying, "It's no big deal." But it is a big deal; one that needs addressing. Coping is simply denial and excusing the severity of your wounds. Those aren't skills—they're crutches.

We break the pain of the past by letting go of anger, bitterness, contempt, and unforgiveness. We embrace the past with acceptance, anticipating that something good will come of it. We let go and let God. This is *dealing* with it.

As I listened to God, the perception of my past began to change. I accepted that not all men are evil; only the ones with evil intent. I accepted that my parents had lived their lives the only way they knew how.

I'm thankful God never gave up on me. The old battle within was ceasing, and a new path to victory began.

WHAT IT'S ALL ABOUT

"If one advances confidently, in the direction of (her) own dreams, and endeavors to lead the life (she) has imagined, (she) will meet with a success unexpected in common hours."

—Henry David Thoreau

Stress

Trauma survivors suffer from the loss of what they once were. They are under severe stress. They have to cope with everyday feelings and needs as well as the reactions of others. Marriage, family life, school, and/or work have been disrupted by the trauma. Their belief that the world was safe has been shattered.

It would be wonderful to wave a magic wand and take away all the grief and loss associated with trauma. There is no magic wand and we can't merely "think" the trauma away. Trauma leaves in its wake anger, grief, and sadness. The reactions of others, who do not understand the trauma of rape and its aftermath, can leave the victim feeling humiliated and guilty.

Rape survivors need love, recognition, and approval. They also need to love and appreciate themselves. Because they lack reinforcement from others, they are often deprived of both. People may be smart, bold, or in good shape, but that doesn't mean they are prepared to face sudden and overwhelming trauma.

Being victimized shocks both your body and your emotions. Research shows that when trauma survivors have someone to turn to, they are less likely to develop Post-Traumatic Stress Disorder.

He heals the brokenhearted and binds up their wounds.
—Psalm 147:3

CHAPTER 7

Perpetrators Change— Well, Some Do

"Be quiet and you won't get hurt," he whispered.

The first time I visited Good Samaritan Ministries, a non-profit Christian mental health clinic, was more than forty years after I was raped. My decision to accept the invitation to sit in on a meeting of recovering sexually assaulted women, male sex offenders, and various other criminals tested my solidarity. After all, I was a wounded veteran of sexual assault. Who could be more authoritative about the subject than I?

My skin crawled as I listened to Joe (not his real name) recount his life of crime in the abuse recovery group. Was I supposed to believe this person could change—a former multiple rapist? Were any of us safe around him? I glared at him as he told his story.

Lurking to the side of a hiking trail in the Columbia River gorge, Joe patiently waited for three approaching women. Soon, they passed by and began to cross a creek single file. Joe seized the last woman. She struggled fiercely, screaming. When the other women joined the chorus of screams, Joe fled.

Like a whipped pup, he turned tail, got in his car, and drove a few miles to another trail head. He waited. Soon, an old woman and a young girl wandered down the trail. Joe grabbed the girl. The woman picked up a large tree branch and vigorously hit him over and over. In spite of Joe's hostile threats, the old woman would not give up. Again, he fled.

One sunny day at the Oregon coast, Joe sat in his car getting drunk. A station wagon with four women inside pulled up. They parked their car and proceeded to unload an enormous amount of camping gear. Joe's mind started racing.

He drove to a secluded spot down the road, and then walked back as dusk was falling. Joe stalked the women as they set up camp in a nearby wind cave. *Perfect*, he thought as two of them headed his way. When they were close enough, he plowed into the two, knocking them to the ground. They struggled briefly, but stopped when they realized he held a gun to one of their heads.

"Be quiet and you won't get hurt," he growled.

Pausing, he wondered what to do next. He had to think fast; the other two women were advancing toward him.

One of the two women he'd captured, a powerful-looking brunette, looked straight in his eyes and said, "What do you think you're doing?"

"I can do whatever I want since I'm the one with the gun."

Without missing a beat, the woman helped her friend up.

"Stop messing around or I'll shoot," Joe ordered.

"Get out of here and leave us alone," the woman screamed. "If you don't, I'll cram that gun right up your nose."

Confused, shocked, and dumbfounded, Joe fled—again.

But Joe persisted. And he finally met with success. Eventually he raped a woman. Then he went on to rape others. All together, his kidnappings, gun possessions, and rapes netted him an exorbitant amount of years in prison. Of course, due to technicalities and a plea bargain, he only served a fraction of his sentence.

At the counselor's prodding, Joe told the group about his childhood. Like many perpetrators, it was miserable. Seeking friendship, he escaped his abusive home life by visiting two older men next door. They treated him well and were generous with their beer and smokes. Then one day, the two guys said to the eleven-year-old boy, "We've been nice to you; now it's time for you to pay us back."

What are they talking about? Joe wondered. He soon found out. The men raped him.

Joe didn't tell anyone for fear no one would believe him. Sadness, confusion, and thinking errors took hold. His life was changed forever.

Before being released from prison, Joe spent many months in treatment for sex offenders at a state hospital. While there he realized he had terrorized all of his victims. He vowed never to harm another woman.

His decision was dramatically reinforced when he was placed in a victim's confrontation session. Seeing so much pain on the faces of survivors caused him to remember the hours of terror he'd experienced as a youth. It made him see how ugly and hideous he had become.

Joe found his way to our abuse recovery group and began regular attendance, submitting himself to accountability. He grew spiritually, reinforcing his choice to change his thinking errors.

However, Joe usually left the group meetings early. He had a hard time sitting through an entire class. He couldn't stand to hear the painful words—they hit too close to home, both as a childhood victim and as a perpetrator.

Survivors Forgive—They Really Do

Joe was particularly moved with compassion toward a woman I'll call Sue.

Sue grew up in an unsafe home that was always filled with violence. Her father was a mean, vicious, cruel man. Her earliest memories are of her father flying into rages and beating her mother. Soon, he began beating Sue.

As the family grew, her brothers and sister were drawn into the circle of beatings. She learned very young how to read her father's face and would react by taking her brothers and sister outside or into another room so they wouldn't get beaten. He instilled such terror in them that little brother would wet his pants whenever Dad walked by. Many times, Sue would step up to interfere with their beatings, and she in turn received what was meant for them.

They were taught to lie about their bruises. They were taught to protect him. They lived in constant fear for their lives.

Her childhood was lonely. When people found out about the violence in her home, their children were not allowed to visit. That made Sue think her family was weird, or that something was wrong with her.

Sue's father also sexually molested her, threatening to kill her and her mother if she told anyone. She didn't tell—until now.

When Sue first came to the abuse recovery group, she sat there, petrified. She trembled and cried, barely able to speak her name. Bettie, the group leader, spoke for her and held her hand throughout the entire session. Sue always positioned herself by other survivors, which made her feel safe.

In class, Sue learned that perpetrators were human and that all of them had been victims of abuse too. Their stories were so similar to her own; these people could have been one of her brothers or sister. Compassion entered her heart. When Sue finally got the nerve to share her story, Joe got up and left the room.

She wrote her dad a letter, expressing grief over her childhood. But he passed away before responding to it. She read the letter to our group. After that, forgiveness filled her heart. She was free from the past, bringing peace at last.

Joe was so touched by Sue's letter, he wrote her one. He wrote what he believed Sue's dad would write if he had lived long enough to respond to her letter. It read something like this:

To my daughter Sue:

I don't know where to begin, Sue, but I am writing this with the hope that you will finally, after so many years and my passing, find some closure for the pain in your heart and soul that you suffered at my hands.

My Sue, so much has been shown to me since I left. I come back to you now not to further torment you, but to ask for forgiveness. This is not for me, but for you. I hope in forgiving me you will be able to someday release the pain in your life. The pain you did not deserve nor want.

Your letter caused me deep sorrow for the evil things I did to you. I didn't acknowledge the letter at that time—I couldn't. I could not face the fact that I molested you and robbed you of so much of your life. I did not deserve to have you for my daughter, nor did you deserve to have me as your father and tormentor.

Sue, I am sorry for hurting you, and for never acknowledging my sins to you or validating you as a child in need. Even after you became an adult, I never validated you.

I don't expect anything I say will make things okay. No father has the right to do what I did to you. Your life will never be okay unless you find strength in the Lord.

Sue, there are many things I would take back if I could. I wish I could have been the father you needed me to be for you. I now see myself for what I am, for what I was, and for what I will always remain because I did not do anything to change while I had the chance. Now that chance is lost to me. Yet, if I could speak to you, I would tell you I was terribly wrong, terribly selfish, and terribly abusive.

My daughter, I am so very sorry. If I could pray, Sue, I would pray that you will move through the pain and leave it behind. Find joy and happiness in everything.

I must go now, my daughter. May God be with you always.

—Dad

Although this letter was written by Joe in place of Sue's father, I suggested to Joe that in reality the letter was written for all the women he had abused. He denied it, but I believe in my heart that my theory is correct.

My perception of perpetrators was beginning to change.

"Still in mutual suffering lies the secret of true living. Love's scars is love that knows the sweetness of forgiving."

—Author unknown

WHAT IT'S ALL ABOUT

"All the things one has forgotten scream for help in dreams."

—Elas Canetti

RAPIST PROFILES: There are four types of rapists:

1. **Power Reassurance:** The most common and least violent stranger-to-stranger rapist. This type can be treated.
2. **Anger Assertive:** The second most common and third most violent. Successful treatment is marginal.
3. **Anger Retaliatory:** Third most common and second most violent. Successful treatment is marginal.
4. **Anger Excitation or the Criminal Sexual Sadist:** These men are sexually aroused by torturing their victims and need to have complete control over another person. They are untreatable.

Within the profiles of the rapists are the admitters and the deniers. They do not take responsibility for their actions. They sometimes acknowledge their acts, but justify them with excuses. "She was a loose woman; she enjoyed it; she was a prostitute; she was drunk." All accept no accountability and minimize their violence.

The typical rapist is nothing more than an aggressive, hostile person who never grew up and chooses to do violence.

I am the Lord, who heals you.

—Exodus 15:26

CHAPTER 8

Tough Love

"To forgive is human, to forget . . . divine."
—James Grant c.1980

I learned about tough love by attending the weekly three-hour abuse recovery group where survivors and perpetrators congregated together. Talk about electricity in the air! Rapists, pedophiles, robbers, and an assortment of other offenders (most on parole) had a chance to hear the emotional damage done to the survivors of their abuse. No thoughts, feelings, or words were held back. Survivors cried, cursed, and eventually some were able to forgive.

Many perpetrators were horrified at the pain they had inflicted upon others. It caused them to think differently about their crimes. For months I listened to their stories. I was amazed!

Forgiveness from survivors came because they were able to face perpetrators and hear their own stories of horror. No, we did not excuse or condone their hideous acts of crime, but we learned what led them into their destructive lifestyle.

As Gavin DeBecker says in his book *The Gift of Fear,* "A difficult childhood excuses nothing, but explains many things."[1]

I remember another particular abuse recovery meeting where several men and women, no more than a few feet apart, gathered. One woman in her late forties, whom I'll call Jennifer, had a concentrated expression of hate, fear, and defiance on her face, directed at a former rapist and ex-convict who sat across the circle from her (whom I'll call Darren). A slender man in his early fifties with thoughtful grey eyes, Darren explained that he had been out of prison for six years after serving seven years of a twelve-year sentence.

All sex offenders are required by law to attend abuse recovery classes while on parole. Darren's turn-around began when he started attending these classes. According to Bettie P. Mitchell, founder and director of Good Samaritan Ministries, their abuse treatment program is the only one of its kind in the United States (to their knowledge). In 1977, she began a treatment program for offenders to meet in a group with adult victims of verbal, physical, and sexual abuse. The purpose is to help offenders and victims to communicate with one another and to work through the long-standing resentments, emotional disfiguration, and suffering that come about from abuse and rape attacks.

Darren told his story of growing up as a troubled child in a home without any sense of order. He had been a small, fragile child. His older brothers picked on him mercilessly, and there was never anyone around to intervene. When he was about nine years old, the family home burned down and his parents divorced. Darren stayed with his mother, who was never around to fulfill her role of maternal guidance.

After his mother remarried, his stepsisters exposed him to sexual play. Through high school, Darren lived with his father. After graduation, he enlisted in the military. When he finished his hitch, he married his high school sweetheart, who was pregnant with another man's child. That marriage did not survive. Neither did the next one.

When Darren married his third wife, she brought three stepdaughters into the union.

He had deviant sex with them, and when it was discovered, he was convicted of statutory rape and sentenced to twelve years in the state penitentiary.

While he was in prison, Darren made a decision. He chose to change his thinking and his behavior. But who could help him make this change? He felt powerless to change himself; sexual addiction is one of the most powerful urges in humans. He wanted to be free of sexually abusive behavior, but the desire was overwhelming. He devised mental games to avoid obsessing, but they weren't successful.

During his time in prison, treatment programs for sex offenders were minimal, and psychological therapy at the state hospital was almost nonexistent. Darren decided that since there was no one to come to the inmates with a recovery agenda, they would have to help themselves. So he started a Bible study in the prison courtyard as well as a sex offender's recovery program. It began with two men and soon grew to sixteen.

After seven years in prison, Darren was released on parole. He was required to participate in an abuse recovery group, which led him to Good Samaritan Ministries in 1997.

While Darren spoke, Jennifer stared at him with hate, fear, and disgust in her eyes from the "safe" side of the room, where she sat close to a counselor she knew. She could not hide the repulsion in her face.

Finally, unable to contain her rage any longer, Jennifer screamed at him, "How could you be allowed to be in this room? You don't deserve to be here. You're not even human."

Darren stood, his eyes filled with sorrow and compassion, and stepped across the room to comfort her.

She shrank away from him as if he were contagious. "You terrify me. Get out of here! I can't sit in this class with you."

Jennifer's counselor advised Darren to return to his seat. Then she convinced Jennifer to stay, and as she continued to glare at him, Darren quietly concluded his story with a brief description of the rape for which he was convicted and sentenced. Then discussion was opened to all individuals in the group.

One woman asked, "Do you think group sessions like this strengthen your resolve to—you know—not sexually assault another woman again?"

"Yes, they do," Darren said slowly. "I've learned that sexually addicted people like me are hard to cure. We're like alcoholics who always have thoughts of liquor somewhere in the back of their minds. Most rapists, even those who've been convicted of sex crimes, repeat them. God helped me when there was nothing I could do to help myself. Groups like this are great for people like me, even though I know they're rough on the women who come, because they're reminded, when they look at us, of the man who did the worst thing to them they could think of."

Encouraged by the compassionate silence that filled the room, Darren continued.

"Another thing that's helpful in group therapy is learning about why you did what you did. You can hear stories of others, and offenders have a chance to talk about themselves and let go of bottled-up feelings."

Perhaps the most valuable benefit from the abuse recovery group is the opportunity for offenders and victims to sit face to face and listen to others describe episodes of terror or reform in their lives. To hear a convicted rapist confess to his crippling sexual confusion is a shock, a vindication, and a revisitation to the terror that originally overwhelmed a victim.

This was certainly the case with Jennifer. Tough love is the path to healing, but it isn't always pleasant to participate in group therapy.

Darren had been a victim as well as an offender. He needed to be healed from his childhood pain and learn how to forgive others and himself. During the many group sessions he attended, he learned how to ask for forgiveness. He discovered more about the healing power of God and how to hold on to his life-changing vows. He knew he would be tempted to slide back into his old ways, and he learned how to resist regression.

But despite his personal progress, Jennifer—plodding treacherously through her own valley of shadows and groping for the light—could not accept his new reality. She spoke harshly to him, making it apparent that she didn't consider him worthy of her forgiveness.

Darren made another vow: to prove to her that he had changed. Over the next few months, Jennifer witnessed Darren's spiritual growth while she sought her own restoration in God. Her heart eventually softened. The positive changes he saw in her made him more determined to succeed than ever.

One day Darren received a letter from Jennifer. It said:

Dear Darren:
I wanted to say thank you for that night when you reached out to me and I pulled away. It was a hard night for

me. It was painful, yet healing at the same time. I've had to remind myself it was okay—you are not the one who hurt me so long ago. But you look so much like him! For a split second, I wanted you to say, "I'm sorry I hurt you." I wanted you to say, "I'll stop the madness now and give back your soul I took so long ago." I wanted you to say, "It was wrong . . . I will stop hurting you now." Then I realized you could not do that; you are not him.

With your continued care and comfort, healing began to stir within me.

Once you were a sex offender, but you've changed. Now you are a man who cares and knows pain . . . not my pain, but your own.

I don't really know what I'm trying to say. Maybe this note is stupid. I just want you to know that I was okay with you tonight, and that I see a good man inside. I never thought I would see or say that about you, or anyone else in the abuse recovery group. I guess that's what healing is all about. I guess that's what this group is all about.

Now I want to say, "Thank you. Thank you for helping me find a piece of healing."

—Jennifer

Jennifer's childhood was full of so much horror, it seems incredible she didn't split into different personalities to survive the torture she endured. Jennifer learned she could make a choice to heal, or she could choose to stay sick in her hatred for her perpetrators. In order to survive her future, she knew what she had to do. Her choice to heal was not easy. She didn't even know if she wanted to change—the pain was almost unbearable. She had to learn to let go of fear, learn to trust, and forgive others—the hardest challenge of all.

Eventually, forgiveness came and she was finally free. It's only by God's power that we are able to accomplish anything, especially what we believe to be unattainable.

I experienced an incredible change in attitude as I began to see perpetrators through the eyes of God. Compassion and forgiveness crept into my heart. The meetings ended with prayer. It felt eerie to hold the hand of a rapist without feeling rage.

As I started viewing my rapist and all mankind as fellow human beings, made in the image of God, my perception changed.

I wanted others to find the same healing from their wounds and strongholds that I found. I wanted to help them. I enrolled in an intensive two-year lay counseling program at Good Samaritan Ministries, and stayed an additional two years as a volunteer counselor.

WHAT IT'S ALL ABOUT

"The years teach us much which the days never knew."
—Emerson 1844

FLASHING: Flashing (exposing oneself without clothing) and obscene phone calls are forms of violation that have the potential for further assault. These are unwanted intrusions into women's personal space, transforming routine and/or potentially pleasurable activities into unpleasant, upsetting disturbances and often threatening experiences. Many sex offenders began offending as flashers and moved on to sexual assault and rape. I have witnessed three flashers in my lifetime.

OBSCENE PHONE CALLS: Obscene phone calls are an example of verbal violence. Threatening calls or silent calls are invasions of privacy. The phone, which is usually our friend and a source of safety, becomes an accessory to crime, thus leaving women vulnerable to further sexual violation.

In your distress you called and I rescued you, I answered you out of a thundercloud.

—Psalm 81:7

CHAPTER 9

Facing the Enemy

The miracle is not in the healing . . . it is in the asking![1]

Corona, California, 2000: Summer. My eyes strained to see the "painted lady" on the hilltop. She was still there, the pale yellow house hiding behind tall trees that had been planted more than thirty-five years ago.

Like a criminal returning to the scene of the crime, I went for a face-off where my rape, divorce, and mental breakdown had taken place. Feeling liberated from past traumas, I wanted to confront my emotions. Had I honestly recovered?

I also wanted to return to the mental hospital and look at my medical records. It would be a challenge, as I had no idea where it was. I didn't even remember the name of the institution.

My children cautioned me not to make the journey. They said I would be sad and disappointed. I should just remember the old place like it used to be. "Besides," they said, "unpleasant memories could surface, perhaps setting you back."

Certain in my plans, and hoping my children would be proven wrong, I continued with the venture.

My niece Vicki agreed to take a day off from work and join me. Locating the old house was easy. But it looked different. Everything seemed dry, dirty, and bleak. The old horse corrals and barns were gone as well as a couple of neighboring homes. A few new ones dotted the landscape.

"Vicki, I heard that a strange single man now lives in the house," I said. "Maybe it's my perpetrator. You should go to the door first," I teased.

"That's fine with me," she said. "I'm not afraid of anyone."

Slowly, we got out of the car and cautiously looked around. Trees, shrubs, and flowers grew where there was once bare ground. We tried to casually look inside, curious to see but afraid of who might appear. Even though a truck sat in the driveway, nobody came to the door when we knocked. Old shovels leaned against the front door, along with well-worn rubber boots and a couple of buckets.

Strange, I thought. *Why would anybody need rubber boots in this hot, dry place? Maybe they're worn to prevent rattlesnake bites.*

I searched the valley below for the enemy's house. It was gone—vanished along with the perpetrator, his daughter, and his mother. I wondered about them. Was the daughter happy? Was the mother dead? Where was he? What evil spirit held that family in bondage?

I wandered off by myself to look around.

Voices

I thought I heard voices from the playhouse stairs
but when I looked, no one was there.
I turned and back to work I went, when again
I heard songs, oh so fair.
I stood very still and strained to listen to a tune
from olden times.
Memories came back of children singing Sunday
school songs and nursery rhymes.

—*L. R. S.*

I stared at the area that once held a playhouse for the girls, and saw them playing in the little house their father had so carefully built. Also, there were the dogs running and howling as beagles do.

I gazed at the large expanse of flat ground carved into the hillside that once was our riding arena and saw myself training my beautiful white Arabian stallion, War Prince. Around and around he would canter, following my commands.

I saw myself riding my first Arabian mare, Rokkessa, bareback around the arena. Her damp copper coat was warm and sticky to my bare legs. She was easy to train and always obedient. She melted my heart with her beautiful dish-shaped head and large, liquid brown eyes. When she ran free, she would hold her tail high, and then stop and turn toward me, prancing, as if to say, "Look at me—I'm lovely!"

I saw the girls riding Thunder, a pokey old palomino gelding that never went faster than a walk until the day lightening struck close by, and then he lived up to his name. He ran like 'thunder'!

I once again heard the soft nickers of the horses as I threw them hay and poured oats into their feed buckets. There was

Nanny, our goat, running to catch up with me in my golf cart, and then jump on for a ride to the bottom of the hill where other horses were waiting to be fed.

I scanned the valley below and saw the girls and myself riding through the orange groves, up the mountain, down the ravines, always watchful for rattlesnakes.

I listened intently for night sounds on our intercom as Rokkessa was ready to deliver her first foal. The splash of her water breaking alerted me. I grabbed my flashlight and ran to her stall. The soft glow of light, the smell of wet straw and sweat from her laboring filled me with awe as a miracle was about to take place, the first of many to follow.

I remember the morning I came back into the house after feeding the horses and found one of the beagles had eaten a dozen donuts and half a loaf of bread. She didn't get fed that night.

I relived trying to grab baby pigs running all over the hillside, having escaped their pens—chasing the neighbor's cows from my yard, who had also escaped their pens—running fiercely to catch up with War Prince, who was eager to get to the mares. He too, had escaped his pen.

I recalled the soft chirps of baby chicks huddled together under a heat lamp as the girls and I stood by in awe.

I could only imagine what life would have been like, had it not stopped at that place in time.

I began to mourn.

I mourned the life I would never have again: exciting moments with the animals, treasured times with the girls. I mourned the loss of my first marriage. I mourned the loss of the life that once was, and never will be again.

At that moment, I wondered what my life would have been like had I not been raped, had someone come, put their arms around me and said, "Please Leila, don't give up. Please Leila, let me help. Let me walk with you through this. Let me pray you through this."

Maybe some did. If they did, I don't remember. Apparently, those who knew me only *thought* they knew me. They didn't recognize my increasing depression as a form of mental illness.

It takes years to recover. It goes in spurts. Recover, feel good. Step back, feel bad. Recover, feel good. Step back, feel bad. On and on it goes, but it always gets better, less painful—until forty years later I wake up one morning crying, wondering *"Why am I crying now?"* Then I realized my mourning wasn't complete, just buried.

My children were right, unpleasant memories did surface, but not the ones they were thinking. What should have been pleasant memories, fun times with the animals, children and husband, became unpleasant memories reminding me of what I had lost. Yes, I was sad; yes, I still felt anger at the rapist for disrupting our once happy life.

Yes, I'm human.

Yes, I know ugly thoughts will surface from time to time. I know I might experience an occasional 'meltdown,' like the time, thirty years after the rape, with no prior warning, I screamed and fell upon my husband's shoulder in the movie theatre, sobbing.

We were watching A Beautiful Mind. It was about a schizophrenic man in a mental hospital. He was on the floor being laced into a straight jacket. His *eyes* pleaded, "Help me, somebody! Help me!" It was at that moment, *he* became *me.* Up to then, I hadn't thought much about my time in the mental hospital, or at least *I didn't think* I had. But, something inside snapped; I needed to mourn that season of my life, also. After my 'encounter of the awful kind' in the movie theatre, I felt a sense of release.

I knew my God was great. He was my Healer. He was my Comforter. He was my hope for a better tomorrow. I knew He would continue to heal me. I stood face to face with my past, mourned it, and looked forward to God's purpose for my future.

> *Don't give up on me.*
> *Please accept me today for who I am*
> *and how far I have come from*
> *Yesterday.*
> *To know I have your acceptance,*
> *love and encouragement gives me*
> *strength, hope and desire for*
> *Tomorrow.*
> *Please don't give up on me.*
> *God hasn't . . .*
>
> *—L. R. S.*

Vicki and I drove down rutted dirt roads in the area, searching for familiar landmarks.

The little Mexican café and beauty salon were nowhere in sight. The turkey ranch and most of the orange groves were gone. "Home" was no longer there; things will never be the same again.

Arriving in town, we began searching for my old hide-away: the mental hospital. The first place we found was "the one." I didn't recognize the name, though. The parking lot was gone, and the building appeared smaller than I remembered.

Entering the lobby, I felt a familiar sense of belonging. The admittance counter was right where I thought it would be. After what seemed like a long time, a woman finally appeared. I introduced myself and told her my reason for being there. She gazed coolly at me, apparently uninterested in my pursuit. With the aloofness of an afghan hound, she tossed her head and said, "I'm sorry, madam, but it's against company policy to let strangers wander the halls without prior permission."

"Please?" I begged. "I won't bother anyone. I only want to reacquaint myself. It will be of great benefit for my book."

She stared at me for several moments. I was about to give up trying to convince her when she motioned me to follow. I scurried through the doorway, giving her no chance to change her mind.

This time, as I followed the nurse with the jangling keys, I wasn't in a daze. I was clear-headed, drinking in all the surroundings. Yes—there was the nurse's station, just where I remember it. The pill-popping place dubbed Poppies. *Tiny*, I mused.

"Is the conference room around the corner?" I asked.

"It is, madam."

All right! I knew this was the right place.

As I walked the narrow halls on cracked linoleum floors, familiar odors floated into my nostrils. Eerie sounds, ones I was well acquainted with, rang mournfully against the stained walls beneath dreary lighting. The outdoor patio was minimal, and sparse of landscaping. I must have been really sick to think I enjoyed myself in that pitiful garden; I was probably desperate for fresh air.

Trotting hastily behind the nurse, I asked, "May I see my medical records?"

She let out a deep sigh. "I'm sorry, madam. We only keep them twenty-five years; after that, they're destroyed."

Drat! I should have made this trip five years ago.

Though her answer was disappointing, I was not discouraged. I was, however, amazed. Did I look and act like these patients when I was there? Void of expression, lifeless, slow to move? How did I endure such a dismal atmosphere for so long? It wasn't awful—just isolated and depressing. I didn't realize how sick I was then.

I had the answer to the question I came for: "Had I honestly recovered?" No, not completely, but I wasn't worried, because "He who began a good work in [me] will *carry it on* to completion until the day of Christ Jesus" (Phil. 1:6).

Had I forgiven my perpetrator? By God's grace . . . yes.

Do I still hate him? No . . . not any longer.

I journeyed to the past, closed the door behind me, and looked forward to the future with sweet anticipation.

[There is] a time to search and a time to give up.
—Ecclesiastes 3:6

Once Upon A Horse

She spoke to me in the aloneness of my silent
world, bright star of my life.
Her copper coat gleamed in the blinding sun,
her muzzle smelling so sweet,
taking me away on phantom journeys.
Flying over green fields and swollen streams,
damp velvet blanket of rippling muscles
soft beneath my skin.
The rhythm of her hoofbeats rang music in my
ears. Her tail flew high, bringing
me safely home again.
Pushing her head into my face, nickering softly
begging for oats, her dark liquid eyes gazed at me.
Oh to feel the magic one more time of
riding the wind upon my horse . . .
. . . once upon my horse again.
—L.R.S.

WHAT IT'S ALL ABOUT

"We crucify ourselves between two thieves: regret for yesterday and fear for tomorrow."

—Fulton Oursler

Suicidal Thoughts: To some survivors, living is viewed as more painful than dying.

Suicidal thoughts are intense feelings of despair. You feel hopeless. But you survived your assault; you will survive your recovery. Every city has suicide-prevention centers and twenty-four-hour hotlines. Your life is worth a phone call. Seek help—you have everything to live for. Sign a suicide contract with your counselor, trusted friend, or family member that you won't harm yourself—that you will call one of them if you are feeling out of control. If suicidal thoughts persist, depression may be the culprit. Seek a psychiatrist for counseling and perhaps an anti-depressant.

Promiscuity: While not a symptom of Post-Traumatic Stress, promiscuity can result from having been raped. Feelings of worthlessness, lack of self-esteem, and devaluing oneself often lead to promiscuity. Rape survivors willing to address this issue with a counselor can be free of this devastating side effect.

Free yourself from the chains around your neck, O' captive daughter of Zion.

—Isaiah 52:2

CHAPTER 10

Do We Ever Recover?

"The God of Mercy pierced my spirit, making me a poster child for His grace."

—L. R. S.

Portland, Oregon, 2001: Summer. Pain never comes without a price. Memories linger in the depths of our souls, and the scars will not completely disappear. However, they can bear witness to God's unfailing love; He can create new life.

Our brokenness can cause us to turn our wills and our lives over to God. We can give Him our sorrows and trust He will make us whole. Smedes says, "Will we let our pain hang on to our hearts where it will eat away our joy? Or will we use the miracle of forgiving to heal the hurt we didn't deserve?"[1]

One night after an abuse recovery meeting, a lady came to me and said that her husband traveled a lot. She was afraid the same thing would happen to her that happened to me. She was afraid her home would be invaded. I told her I couldn't guarantee that wouldn't happen, but I assured her she didn't have to be bound by fear. I told her to claim Psalm 4:8, "I will lie down and sleep in peace, for You alone, O Lord, make me dwell in safety." I told her to put the scripture under her pillow.

Another friend told me her perpetrator was due to be released from jail soon. She confided that she was afraid he might try to find her. I prayed for her, and then told her she didn't have to be bound by fear. Psalm 18:2 says, "The Lord is my rock, *my fortress* and *my deliverer*; my God is *my rock,* in whom I *take refuge.* He is *my shield* and the horn of my salvation, my stronghold."

We live in a fallen world where evil reigns. Bad things happen. Life isn't fair. I cannot promise you'll never be assaulted. I cannot promise you'll never be assaulted *again.* I can only pray to God you won't be. We cannot eliminate the *cause* of fear, but we don't have to let it control our lives.

Bruce Larson, in his book *Living Beyond Our Fears,* says, "Fear is the handle by which we lay hold on God. The opposite of fear is faith. When you stop running and face your fear head on with faith, you find God. It is His presence and power that move us beyond our fears—past, present and future."[2]

No one knows the future accurately except God. For us, it's unpredictable, and that scares us.

Fear is the most crippling disease known to mankind. It can be the driving force in our perception of life. But we can trust God for the future because He's already there.

Adversity strengthens us, instilling confidence to handle other crises that may come our way. Despite the pain and devastation that come with any trial, it can guide us toward maturity and inner healing. Something good will come of it. I'm not saying I want bad things to happen in order to learn about good outcomes! But I know good will prevail in spite of bad.

Luis Palau said, in his book *Where Is God When Bad Things Happen?,* "There will always come a time (or more likely, times) when tragic events invade our lives, bearing no trace of God's purposes and no hint of rational explanation. What do we do in those times? The only thing we can do. We trust in the character of a loving God, a righteous God, a holy and compassionate God, who always does right. We will not always understand His ways, but can always trust His character. That is the ultimate conviction that must sustain all of us, even when the answers we seek to life's tragedies escape our most searching gaze."[3]

Perception: A Key Factor in Recovery

Brenda Gates Smith says, "Every person has defining moments that tint their world like colored glasses, a lens through which they filter other moments, creating a foundation for self perception." Each individual is a unique human being graced with God's personal blueprint, unlike any other.

Everyone perceives life differently, making reasoning our sole personal agenda. Perception is a key factor in recovery. Generally, it isn't the trauma itself that sends us into a spin, but our perception of it.

By allowing God to change my perception, I learned to deal with intrusive, negative thoughts of the past by dismissing them with positive ones . . . most of the time. I learned to forgive and *not* forget, lest I return to the angry, bitter woman I was. I must renew my faith daily so the evil one (Satan) doesn't test me in a weak moment and try to destroy my newfound freedom.

However, I haven't "arrived." While I still don't trust everyone, that doesn't mean I don't trust anyone. It's okay to be suspicious of some people and not consider myself paranoid. A little dose of woman's intuition doesn't hurt either.

For most of us, recovery is a gradual process. It moves silently, unsuspectingly, drawing us closer to peace with each advancing year. Rape survivors ask me, "What's the plan? Do you have a twelve-step program? I want to get started right away and be recovered by next Christmas." But recovery doesn't work that way. Recovery comes from maturing in our thinking, a turn-around in our perception. We must cease blaming others and forgive those who have inflicted pain in our lives. Recovery comes to us in the light of education, learning, and understanding evil.

As I reach far back in time, my memory dims; dates and events blur together, making me wonder, *Did that really happen?* Then out of nowhere, something occurs to awaken memories inside my head: a dream, an event, something someone did or said. And I am reminded once again of a long-lost past that springs to life, linking itself to the present.

Recovery from trauma can be a lifetime process. Just when we think we have recovered, something happens that rattles our cage. But we can reach out, take hold of the cage, and steady it. Remembering how far we have come will remind us of how far we can go.

I hope you have a clearer understanding of evil, its origin, and its effect on humankind. "The great dragon was hurled down—that ancient serpent called the devil, or Satan, who leads the whole world astray" (Rev. 12:9). He and his angels represent evil, are evil, do evil, and their mission is to destroy humankind, especially through our minds. That's why the world is in a mess and people commit evil. But remember, just because *one* man sexually assaulted you (maybe you had more than one) doesn't mean *all* men are evil. Don't let your heart harden. If it has, ask God to give you a new heart: one free of hate and bitterness.

We can let evil acts destroy us, or we can, with God's help, triumph over them. I know the discernment of evil doesn't dissolve the impact of our traumas. However, enlightenment can help turn our perception around and soften our hearts, making it easier to forgive. It has for me.

One morning a few years ago, I stumbled into a men's Bible study at my home. When the visitors asked how I was, I replied, "Fine, except for my nightmares." I was immediately surrounded. They laid hands on me and asked God to free my mind from those night terrors.

After they prayed, I said, "Thanks, guys," and went about my day. Ever since that prayer was prayed over me, I have never had a single *nightmare* from the past.

The prophecy of celebrating something special in six months came to pass. A move back to the Portland area found my husband and me observing Christmas with our family—exactly six months from the date of the prophecy!

After six years of taking anti-depressants, I decided not to let a pill control my happiness. I needed to be responsible for my own emotions, at least in part. During the six years I took anti-depressants, they gave me the ability to see life with clarity. I was able to process my thoughts in an orderly fashion. Panic attacks, anxiety, and depression ceased. However, my hair fell out, I gained weight, and with one medication, I passed out. It was time to quit taking them. Stopping wasn't easy . . . I struggled. However, the longer I went without medication, the less I was depressed.

Depression still knocks at my door occasionally, but I don't reach for a pill, I reach for God. I pray—even if I don't feel like it. I know it sounds too simple, but try it. It worked for me; it just might work for you, too.

I'm not suggesting everyone go off their anti-depressants. They are vital for some people, making the difference between life and death. However, for those who want to quit taking anti-depressants, support groups, cognitive therapy, and the power of Jesus Christ can help you manage and even overcome depression. (Always check with your doctor before going off medication. Some medications should not be stopped abruptly.)

Life can pour down on us in unexpected ways—some good, some bad. I never dreamed my rape would carry me away to the pit of hell and that, like the Phoenix, I would rise up to a life of wholeness.

I have forgiven my perpetrator and my parents. I no longer look at men with disdain. I am free from the strongholds that bound me to the past. And now, I can forgive myself.

If freedom from strongholds (past or present) is your desire, with God's help, you can recover from your pain. You can be free from the power of darkness that binds you to the past. Ask God for wings to fly away from the strongholds that are keeping you grounded. Ask Him to give you the promise He gave me: *I will bring peace to your life like the calm on the morning pond.* Invite Him to journey with you. Trust Him; you won't be sorry.

Each one of us has a purpose in life. God has a plan for you, and your reason for being is included in that plan. We need not waste our sorrows; we are to use the pain that comes into our lives to help others overcome their pain. We can give love, hope, and encouragement. As you seek and trust God, your reason for being will most likely be revealed.

We live in the now, not in the past or the future. So make the most of today and leave tomorrow to God. Life will always be ragged around the edges, but it goes on.

Time does not heal all wounds of the heart. Only the power of God's Son, Jesus Christ, with His infinite love, can make all things beautiful. "He has made everything beautiful in its time" (Eccl. 3:11).

Invite Jesus Christ into your heart. He is your Comforter and Healer. He will make everything beautiful for you in His time. I know—He has for me.

Awesome blessings!

—Leila Rae.

He will bring to light what is hidden in darkness and will expose the motive of men's hearts.

—1 Corinthians 4:5

WHAT IT'S ALL ABOUT

"The past I have placed in God's keeping. For the present
His grace doth appear and what seems so dark in the future
will brighten as I draw near."

—Author unknown

Finding New Meaning and Structure in Life

Rape changes the view of the world in the eyes of the victim.
She sees life and people differently. However, challenging as
it seems, it is an opportunity to make positive changes. While
sorrow is one of life's greatest tragedies, it is not purposeless.
Finding meaning in her sorrow will help her forge a new self.
In doing so, she will be molded into a much different person
bringing strength and beauty. Supportive friends and family
can take part in that new birth, cheering her on so that her
sorrow will have meaning.

"Though afflicted, tempest-toss'd,
Comfortless a while thou art,
Do not think thou canst be lost,
Thou are graven on My heart.
All thy waste I will repair,
Thou shalt be rebuilt anew;
And in thee it shall appear
What a God of love can do."

—Author Unknown

Part 2
A Biblical, Historical, and Social Perspective About Rape

Eve allowed herself to be deceived by the serpent.
—L.R.S.

CHAPTER 11

Mother Eve

"Eve was not an afterthought of God."

—L.R.S.

Genesis, the first book of the Holy Bible, means "origin, source, or beginning." Genesis is the book of origins. It gives a majestic account of the beginnings of all the Creator brought into being. Genesis takes the reader back to the all-important moment of creation when the omnipotent Creator spoke into being the matchless wonders of sun, moon, stars, planets, galaxies, plants, moving creatures, and man—the one whom He made in His image.[1]

The NIV *Matthew Henry Bible Commentary* says, "The Holy Scripture by revealed religion lays down, at first, this principle that this world was in the beginning of time, created by a Being of infinite wisdom and power, who was Himself before all, and all worlds. God the Father Almighty is the Maker of heaven and earth."[2]

The idea of woman's inferiority goes back to Genesis; more precisely, to two episodes on which many theologians have commented.

First, God created Eve from Adam. In the minds of many theologians this fact justifies woman's submission to man. The account of Eve's creation from Adam's rib, a curved bone, even indicated to some that the mind of woman was twisted and perverse.

Second, Satan tempted Eve, and Eve seduced Adam, leading him into sin.[3] Eve allowed herself to be deceived by the ancient serpent, a snake known as Satan. The result? Eternal damnation, sin, and death. Adam and Eve's disobedience left a devastating horror to reverberate on humankind—forever.

According to *The History of Women, Vol. II*, men thought Eve's fatal weakness made her particularly vulnerable and guilty. She was considered the source of all evil. All women who succeeded her were the same, except for the virgin Mary.

This negative attitude toward women was unambiguously expressed in a fresco in the Parish Church of San Michele Arcangelo in Paganico (Siena), painted by Bartolo di Fredi, which read: "I am the mortal enemy of all that is good, servant of the devil, woman of hell, mother of eternal pain." It goes on to say, "It was hard for women to overcome or bypass the condition of being born female."[4]

The message the church handed down to its followers, which fed their fantasies and negatively influenced men's views of women and women's views of themselves, was that men were to be treated very differently from women. Men sinned when they misused their capabilities or ideas or when they were unable to control their impulses and sentiments. Nothing was required of women because their bodies led them inexorably toward transgression.[5]

The History of Women, Volume II goes on to say, "The Bible shaped men's ideas. What they perceived of reality was filtered through the prism of Scripture. Or rather, they were convinced that what we call reality is merely a shadow of an idea, the idea of woman, which can be most fully grasped through the study of those texts in which the revelation of all that is true was vouchsafed into man."[6]

A remark made by Gregory of Tours at the Council of Macon in AD 585 lent credence to the idea that clerical thinkers seriously doubted that women have a soul.[7]

Man's body was fashioned by the Lord God from the dust of the ground, while his spirit came from the very "breath" of God. He is literally a creature of two worlds; both earth and heaven can claim him.

Moses, the inspired author of Genesis, alluded to man's loneliness and lack of full satisfaction. But the Creator had not finished. He had plans for providing a companion who would satisfy the unfulfilled yearning of man's heart, created for fellowship and companionship. Man would enter into full life only when he shared love, trust, and devotion in the intimate circle of the family relationship.

Jehovah made it possible for man to have a helpmeet for him. She was to be one who could share man's responsibilities, respond to his nature with understanding and love, and wholeheartedly cooperate with him in working out the plan of God.[8]

God made Eve after Adam. God had created all the animals and let Adam name them. Adam looked at the animals and saw nothing that resembled him or any creature that would give him comfort and fellowship. That is why God made Eve *after* Adam. If Eve had been made at the same time as Adam, he would not have felt lonely or sought companionship. The sequence of events was a purposely divine plan.

This would dismiss the theory passed down by men through the centuries that Eve was an afterthought and inferior. Nothing is an afterthought with God. Eve was a precious daughter of God, created in His image, presented to man to be loved, honored, and cherished.

The *NIV Matthew Henry's Commentary* also says, "Woman was taken not from man's head to rule over him, nor from his feet to be trampled on by him, but out of his side to be equal with him, under his arm to be protected, and close to his heart to be beloved."[9] She is also represented in the story of creation as wholly dependent upon her husband, and not complete without him. Also, man is never fully complete without the woman. It is God's will that it should be so.

The loving heart of God doubtless rejoiced in the institution of a relationship that was to be clean, holy, and pleasant for mankind.[10] However, the pages of history reveal that some men perceived Eve as inferior, the prime instigator of evil, causing the fall of humankind. They used the old theological argument that Adam came first, thus claiming superiority over woman.

For some men, contempt of women through the ages has been used to subordinate, control, kill, rape, and even convict them of witchcraft. They relentlessly flogged them with Scripture abuse in the name of God's holy Word, repeatedly pointing out certain Scriptures to justify their twisted actions.

John Chrystom, (fifth-century Christian teacher) made this prefatory judgment of woman: "The enemy of friendship, the excruciating pain, the necessary evil, the natural temptation, the desirable calamity, the domestic peril, the delectable scourge, nature's woe was painted in bright color."[11] In the Middle Ages, Insitoris and Sprenger called upon their personal experiences as inquisitors and witch hunters. They had observed that woman's rebellious nature and congenital weakness made her susceptible to devilish and evil temptations.

Around AD 1098, Marbode of Rennes declared his contempt for women and the flesh. "Woman," he said, "was a temptress, a sorceress, a serpent, a plague, a vermin, a rash, a poison, a searing flame, and intoxicating spirit."[12]

Women, through whom death, suffering, and toil came into the world, were creatures dominated by their sex. To control and punish women, particularly their bodies and their dangerous disruptive sexuality, was therefore man's work. Scientific, ethical, and political thought converged in the notion that woman must either remain chaste or devote herself solely to procreation. All her functions were directed toward one end: reproduction.[13]

"A mother's primary obligation was to bring offspring into this world, to generate children continually until her death," were the words of Dominica Nicholas of Gorran (who died in AD 1295).[14]

The *Wycliffe Bible Commentary* says, "The author (Moses) represents God as planting a beautiful garden for his new creatures. 'Eden' means an enclosure or a park. The Hebrew word 'Eden' probably means enchantment, pleasure or delight. Man's work in that garden was to exercise dominion while serving . . . a good combination. In this quiet place of indescribable beauty, humankind was to enjoy fellowship and companionship with the Creator, and to work in accord with the divine blueprint to perfect His will."[15]

The Garden of Eden had two extraordinary trees unique to itself. On earth there were no others like them.

In the middle of the garden was the Tree of Life, which was chiefly intended to be a sign and seal to Adam, assuring him of the continuance of life and happiness, even to immortality and everlasting bliss, through the grace and favor of his Maker, on condition of his perseverance in this state of innocence and obedience. Of this he might eat and live forever.

Then there was the Tree of Knowledge of Good and Evil, so called not because it had any virtue in it to beget or increase useful knowledge, but because there was an express positive revelation of the will of God concerning that Tree.

The first purpose of this tree was so that by it man might know moral good and evil. What is good? It is to not eat of this tree. What is evil? It is to eat of this tree. The distinction between all other moral good and evil was written in the heart of man by nature. But God's distinction, which resulted from a positive law, was written on this tree.

Second, the tree gave Adam an experimental knowledge of good by the loss of it, and of evil by the sense of it.

So the covenant of innocence had in it, not only "do this and live," which was sealed and confirmed by the Tree of Life, but also "fail and die."

You may wonder, "Why did God put those trees there?" The answer is simple. God does not want robots for companionship in heaven. He gave us free will to choose.

"God does not force the will or judgment of any. He takes no pleasure in a slavish obedience. He desires that the creatures of His hands shall love Him because He is worthy of love. He would have them obey Him because they have an intelligent appreciation of His wisdom, justice, and benevolence."[16]

The heart of the sons of men is full of evil, and madness is in their heart while they live, and after that they go to the dead.

—Ecclesiastes 9:3 (KJV)

CHAPTER 12

They Do It Because They Want To

> "We are the only creatures on the planet that hunt and kill for pleasure and sport."
>
> —Sean Mactire, Malicious Intent

Violence is a disease. It is referred to in medical terms as "intentional trauma."[1] Violence is not a social or a legal problem. It is a complication of mental illness. Criminals are evil, as we have discovered. It is a constant desire to be childishly self-indulgent. A criminal wishes to do whatever he/she pleases, with nothing but contempt and total disregard for the rights and feelings of others. Like a child, the criminal always wants something for nothing.[2]

Freud once said a child would destroy the world if it had the power. Simply, a child is totally subjective. A child has no desire to consider nor accept the viewpoint of others because a child is incapable of acknowledging anything other than the desire to satisfy his or her own feelings.[3] A criminal is a ruthless adult who never stops behaving like a child—the victim of a chronic disease that makes a person obsessed with taking shortcuts.[4]

In Sean Mactire's book *Malicious Intent,* he says, "Everyone is capable of committing a crime, but other than the petty stuff, the life of crime of most people is limited to their dreams and daytime fantasies. So, what makes the average person so different from criminals? There is no difference. The criminals you read about in your newspaper and see on television are just a reflection of the darkness that dwells within *every* human being."[5]

He goes on to say, "Why did this darkness, the shadow side, come to dominate these people, turning them to a life of crime, and a chosen path of evil, and not you or any of the genuinely decent people of our society? The answer is simple. You and the decent people grew up into mature human beings, and the criminal stagnated in perpetual childhood. This degeneration in behavior is accentuated by three basic traits that signify the criminal personality: (a) weakness, emotional and/or physical, lacking discipline; (b) immaturity, childish egocentrism; (c) self-deception, distorted sense of personal reality, severely narcissistic. Criminals seem to feed on the fear of their victims, feed on the power they derive from their acts, and feed on the pleasure, often sexual, that their acts provide."[6]

Why do some people become diseased with violence and others remain healthy? Mactire says, "The reason is resistance, and deception is the cloak of darkness that the sadistic hunters of the criminal subculture use to hide the pursuit of their chosen prey. Never underestimate or take for granted the potential for human destructiveness that lives within us all.[7]

"Since the dawn of time, human beings have wondered why other humans commit crimes. Humans are the only creatures that can turn anything into a weapon. People may blame guns for violence and criminal behavior, but the reality is that all destructive or nonproductive behavior is motivated by power.

In a nutshell, crime is about power. In the simplest of terms, criminals are parasites.[8]

"Crime is part of a disease cycle that is infectious; it can be anywhere. With their sheer numbers alone, violent criminals, career criminals, and killers of all types are a society and race unto themselves.[9]

"In our society, sex is the most pervasive influence affecting every aspect of our lives. Our modern Western society demands instant gratification and instant relief from boredom."[10]

America has one of the highest rates of rape in the world. It seems to be the all-American crime. No wonder women are always looking over their shoulders. Going out after dark becomes a serious issue. Is it necessary? Running in the park, even with other people, can leave you feeling guarded. Walking up deserted stairs or stepping into an elevator with a solitary man may become a debatable decision.

Rape is the only crime where the victim is regarded as the offender and the only crime for which provocation is an acceptable defense. Rape has been referred to as an "assault with a friendly weapon."

Liz Kelly, in her book *Surviving Sexual Violence,* says, "Women have to find ways of managing the threat of sexual violence. We choose from a range of coping strategies, each of which involves an assessment of risks and costs. The reality of sexual violence remains such a common experience and while women feel that they can expect little protection from others, be they passersby or the police, a sense of vulnerability is a realistic response. It is one of the many costs of this reality that some women are affected so strongly that they choose to limit their lives in dramatic ways."[11]

Men usually are not threatened with evil by women and children. They rarely have to look over their shoulders, keeping watch for an unseen enemy. They leave home, have fun, work, and do all the things men like to do without any anxiety. If men could walk in the shoes of women and children for a year, they might have more compassion for their safety. A world without rape would be a world where women would be free from the fear of men.

> You will go out in joy and be led forth in peace . . . Instead of the thorn bush will grow the pine tree, and instead of the briars, the myrtle will grow.
>
> —Isaiah 55:12-13

CHAPTER 13

Our Fathers' Iniquities

We cannot turn back the clock and put the apple back on the tree.

—L.R.S.

The word *beget* means "1. father, sire, procreate, get; breed, propagate, reproduce; 2. cause, produce, effect, make happen, bring about, bring to pass, give rise to occasion" (*Rodale Synonym Finder*, 1978).[1]A man begets children (fathers them) and women give birth to children. The word *beget* always refers to the male. Not only does he play a role in the part of reproduction, but he can bring about circumstances, producing cause and effect.

Genesis 2:16-17 says, "And the Lord God commanded the man, 'You are free to eat from any tree in the garden; but you must not eat from the tree of the knowledge of good and evil, for when you eat of it you will surely die.'

Now the serpent was more crafty than any of the wild animals the Lord God had made. He said to the woman, "Did God really say, 'You must not eat from any tree in the garden'?"

The woman said to the serpent, "We may eat fruit from the trees in the garden, but God did say, 'You must not eat fruit from the tree that is in the middle of the garden, and you must not touch it, or you will die.'"

"You will not surely die," the serpent said to the woman. "For God knows that when you eat of it your eyes will be opened, and you will be like God, knowing good and evil" (Gen. 3:1-5).

Adam and Eve were given the power of choice.

The book of Genesis goes on to say that Eve took of the fruit and gave some to her husband, Adam, who was with her. Their eyes were opened and they realized they were naked, so they made coverings for themselves. They then proceeded to hide from God, for they were ashamed.

Adam, poor soul, was as pliable as putty; he took the fruit and ate it. His childlike manner shows him to be passive in his act of disobedience. Perhaps he thought he would lose Eve forever if he didn't join her—who knows?

When confronted by God about their sin, neither Adam nor Eve accepted any blame. It was a classic case of "he said, she said." They each blamed others. Eve said, "The serpent deceived me and I ate" (Gen. 3:13). Adam said, "The woman you put here with me, she gave me some fruit from the tree, and I ate it" (Gen. 3:12).

All of them had to pay for their transgressions: the serpent, the man, and the woman. God became prosecutor, judge, and jury.

The Lord God said to the serpent, "Because you have done this, cursed are you above all the livestock and all the wild animals! You will crawl on your belly and you will eat dust all the days of your life. And I will put enmity between you and the woman, and between your offspring and hers; he will crush your head, and you will strike his heel" (Gen. 3:14-15).

To the woman He said, "I will greatly increase your pain in childbearing; with pain you will give birth to children. Your desire will be for your husband, and he will rule over you" (3:16).

To Adam He said, "Because you listened to your wife and ate from the tree about which I commanded you, 'You must not eat of it,' cursed is the ground because of you; through painful toil you will eat of it all the days of your life. It will produce thorns and thistles for you, and you will eat the plants of the field. By the sweat of your brow you will eat your food until you return to the ground, since from it you were taken; for dust you are and to dust you will return" (3:17-19).

Adam and Eve realized that they were out of touch with God, and a terrible loneliness overwhelmed them. Remorse and its inevitable miseries followed. All humanity henceforth would be doomed to struggle in the sea of sin.

I can just imagine the fights that might have taken place after Adam and Eve were banished from Paradise; him blaming her for eating the apple, and her blaming him because he didn't protect her from Satan's temptation. Perhaps that prompted him to ensure that she never made a fatal error again. By tightening the reins, did he believe he could prevent her from stumbling into no good? Maybe tightening the reins began out of fear—fear that she would cause further chaos. Was this the beginning of hard-line beliefs and traditions to control women?

Because I believe the Bible is the infallible Word of God, the fall-from-paradise story is not a myth, as many would have us believe. There are those who believe this story was made up by certain tribes in early biblical times so they could rule women.

When God judged woman, He sentenced her with subjection to the man. She would realize womanly longings and

123

desires, but not without agony. This is woman's penalty for sin and disobedience.

I now have a different attitude toward God's judgment on women. We must accept this sentence. Not to do so is being defiant toward God. While we cannot fully comprehend the nature of God's judgment, we can understand that rebellion leads to grief and sorrow at its worst.

Now, accepting our divine sentence does not mean we are to be treated violently, verbally abused, raped, cheated on, dishonored, or disrespected. Woman's sentence was not intended to bring her to ruin, but to repentance, and to protect her from the way the world is now.

The entrance of sin made that duty a punishment, which otherwise *would not have been*. Though it seems severe, we should not complain. Rebelling against this punishment violates and thwarts a divine law and sentence. Considering our crime against God's protective instructions for humanity, the punishment is deserved.

Let me give you an example of a woman's sentence that may make it clearer to understand. Let's say you were warned time and time again about the abuse of drunken driving, yet continued to drink and drive. Finally, you had a collision that killed a person. Your punishment was to have your driver's license taken away and serve time in jail. When you were released from jail, you were free, but you could not own or drive a car, making you dependent on others for transportation. The judge didn't say you couldn't go and enjoy life; just that you can't drive a car. That was your sentence.

Adam and Eve had to pay for their disobedience; so do we. How else will we learn the consequences of sin, learn right from wrong, and have a desire to do what is good and right? Woman's sentence was subjection to her husband. While we must accept it, it was never intended to be misused. It was a reminder to never forget our disobedience.

Woman's sentence does not mean she cannot be a whole, fulfilled person. It means she is protected by God so she can live unhindered by guilt. She can achieve some of the same aspirations men do: dreams, careers, hobbies, education, own property and/or businesses, fly to the moon, and seek the desires of her heart.

I must confess, there was a time when I could never have agreed with this chapter, much less write it. I would go out of the way to demean men, and in general considered them untrustworthy. A lifetime of harboring a rebellious attitude toward men can be difficult to change.

Sometimes my old attitude tries to delegate my thoughts. I have to stop and bite my tongue so I won't say something I will regret. As I am reminded of God's love, calm and peace find a home in my heart, making it easier to control my emotions.

> I will seek that which was lost, and bring again that which was driven away, and will bind up that which was broken, and will strengthen that which was sick.
> —Ezekiel 34:16 (KJV)

CHAPTER 14

The Ties That Bind

Perhaps Adam was motivated out of fear—fear that Eve would
cause further chaos and take everyone down with her.

—L.R.S.

In the first chapter of *The City of Ladies,* Christine de Pisan
discusses the misfortune of having been born a woman. "In
my folly," she writes, "I despaired that God caused me to be
born in a female body." Her disgust with herself at one time
encompasses all her sex, as if nature had given birth to monsters, and she blamed God. But when she dissected the roots
of her misery, she came to blame her misfortune on a series
of authorities. Men had singled women out as fundamentally
wicked and given to vice. This took place in the Middle Ages,
giving way to the Renaissance, around A.D. 1400.[1]

"If we were to take at their word the men who wielded legal
power over women and heard their confessions, who assailed
them with endless treatises and sermons, we would have no
choice but to conclude that women were ensnared in webs

of rules so constraining that they could not utter a word or move a muscle."[2]

"While the family played an increasingly important part in fifteenth-century culture and ideology, woman, who had always been seen within the context of the family, increasingly was afforded little consideration. Fifteenth-century treatises on the family reveal only one real novelty: the discovery that woman had a soul."[3]

The secular and canon laws written from the thirteenth century on gave husbands primary and social control over their wives. Man, with the firm belief that because woman was born after him, felt justified putting her beneath him, and exercised discipline and punishment.

Most Christian theologians and male leaders had, by the fifth century, orchestrated denigrating views of women: women were inferior, bad, naughty; men were superior, good, propitious. They recommended that women wear veils and men grow beards to intensify the difference between the sexes.

From the second century on, Eve was seen by the Christian church as the source of sin, the temptress of man, and the embodiment of all women. "And do you know that you are (each) an Eve?" wrote Turtullian around AD 200. He goes on to say, "The devil is in you. You broke the seal of the Tree. You were the first to abandon God's law. You were the one who deceived man, whom the devil knew not how to vanquish. It was you who so easily overcame him who was made in the image of God. For your wages you have death, which brought death even to the Son of God."[4]

Merlin Stone, author of *When God Was a Woman,* said that St. John Chrysostom, a Christian teacher of the fifth century AD, had warned, "The woman taught once and ruined everything. On this account, let her not teach."[5]

"St. Augustine, of the same period, *claimed* [italics mine] that man, but not woman, was made in God's image and woman therefore is not complete without man, while he (man) is complete alone."[6] Stone went on to say that Martin Luther (AD 1500) asserted in his writing, "Men must continue to maintain their power over women, since man is higher and better than she, for the regiment and dominion belong to the man as the head master of the house."[7]

During the Montanist period, virgins were reminded "to remain veiled" and told what they could and could not do. Women were not permitted to speak in church, much less teach, make offerings, or claim for themselves any of the functions that properly belong to men, most notably the sacerdotal ministry.[8] Women were required to cover their heads; men were not.

All Feminine Nature Has Thus Fallen into Error

Fourth-century women were prohibited from approaching the altar. During menstruation, deaconesses were allowed to remain in the church but not to approach the altar . . . not because they were impure, but so that the altar could be honored.

By the seventh century, all the myths about the destructive power of menstrual blood had been revived and reasserted. Bishop Isidore of Seville insisted that the touch of a menstruating woman could prevent fruit from ripening and cause plants to die. Pope Gregory the Great commended women who stayed away from the church when they were menstruating, but did not insist they do so.

The History of Women, Vol.1, commented that, "The race of women is weak, fickle, of mediocre intelligence, and an instrument of the devil; how can she aspire to a sacerdotal function?"[9]

From early childhood, males were presented with the message that real men dominate women. They were given permission to control their women's behavior, and could verbally and physically abuse them. The appearance of manhood was so strong in men that their posture of dominance over women when in the presence of other men demanded honor and admiration; the opinion of their peers was very important. Self-esteem could only be achieved by being witnessed by other men.

Childbirth was seen as a contaminating experience. By the end of the sixth century, the Hebrew tradition was that a woman remained unclean for thirty-three days after the birth of a son, sixty-six days after the birth of a daughter. Priests ritually purified a woman after the specified time from the contamination of childbearing and the greater contamination of having given birth to a daughter. Only then could she re-enter the church and participate again as a member of the congregation.

History tells us of dogmatic customs established to the degree of absurdity. Jewish law forbade women to sit with men in the main part of the synagogue. They were separated by a *mihizah* (a partition). Because they considered woman's voice a sexual provocation, they could not read or receive before men.

"Women should not read the Torah because men would be sexually distracted."[10] How would a woman reading the Torah threaten the honor of the congregation? It was highly unlikely it would be read by women anyway, because the rabbis thought it nonsense for fathers to teach their daughters the Torah.

Women's relation to the written word was viewed with suspicion. A woman should learn neither to read nor write, unless she was interested in taking vows, because women's reading and writing has brought many evils.[11] Early Jews repeated this prayer: "Blessed be God for not making me a woman."[12]

Purge Evil from You, O Israel

The Holy Bible has much to say about the laws of marriage. For example:

If a man takes a wife and, after lying with her, dislikes her and slanders her and gives her a bad name, saying, "I married this woman, but when I approached her, I did not find proof of her virginity," then the girl's father and mother shall bring proof that she was a virgin to the town elders at the gate.

The girl's father will say to the elders, "I gave my daughter in marriage to this man, but he dislikes her. Now he has slandered her and said, 'I did not find your daughter to be a virgin.' But here is the proof of my daughter's virginity."

Then her parents shall display the cloth before the elders of the town, and the elders shall take the man and punish him. They shall fine him a hundred shekels of silver and give them to the girl's father, because this man has given an Israelite virgin a bad name.

She shall continue to be his wife; he must not divorce her as long as he lives.

If, however, the charge is true and no proof of the girl's virginity can be found, she shall be brought to the door of her father's house and there the men of her town shall stone her to death. She has done a disgraceful thing in Israel by being promiscuous while still in her father's house. *You must purge the evil from among you.*

If a man is found sleeping with another man's wife, both the man who slept with her and the woman must die. *You must purge evil from Israel.*

If a man happens to meet in a town a virgin pledged to be married and he sleeps with her, you shall take both of them to the gate of that town and stone them to death—the girl because she was in a town and did not scream for help, and the man because he violated another man's wife. *You must purge the evil from among you.*

But if out in the country a man happens to meet a girl pledged to be married and rapes her, only the man who has done this shall die. Do nothing to the girl; she has committed no sin deserving death.

If a man happens to meet a virgin who is not pledged to be married and rapes her and they are discovered, he shall pay the girl's father fifty shekels of silver. He must marry the girl, for he has violated her. He can never divorce her as long as he lives" (Deut. 22:13-29, emphasis mine).[13]

Man-made laws of biblical times are still in use today in many countries. Even today, some men regard women as chattel. Women still need a dowry. And the husband may divorce her by saying, "I divorce you" three times.[14]

Sandra Mackey says, in her book *Saudis: Inside the Desert Kingdom*, "Arab ethics revolve around a single focal point; the personal honor of the man. Man's vaunted honor depends on the sexual behavior of the women for whom he is responsible. Arab men live in terror that their women will commit a sexual offense. They decree that a woman can lose her sexual honor by doing something as seemingly chaste as sitting next to a man on an airplane. And once lost, her sexual honor can never be regained. In truth, it is the man's honor that is at stake. The Saudi's preoccupation with female sexual chastity is an obsession."[15]

There are more rules for these women: No travel outside Saudi Arabia without written permission of the senior male member of her family. She cannot leave her house without permission or go out alone. She can speak to no man except relatives. Men usually do the shopping and most of the errands. (Women are not allowed to drive a car.) She must remain veiled in public and wear special clothes so that a man cannot become sexually aroused by her. She is not allowed in public places where men congregate. Her menstrual cycle condemns her as unclean (meaning she cannot go to the mosque). Marriages are arranged, and the husband makes all the decisions for the family. The husband may have as many as four wives, plus concubines, and all are saddled with numerous other do's and don'ts.

"The purpose of keeping women in seclusion is to protect their chastity, and their value. The worth of a woman in Saudi culture is as breeding stock to increase the size and the strength of the husband's family. In the Saudi mind, the sexual drive of women can only be controlled by a strict code of conduct, while the strong sex drive of men is socially acceptable."[16]

A man's honor resides in the number of sons he begets, as it is his sign of male virility. Society and religion have decreed that the role for women was wife and mother.

"Saudis view women primarily as sex objects whose destiny is to serve and obey.

It is instilled early, even before the weaning process begins. For instance, boys are breast-fed much longer than girls, often for as long as two to three years. The pampering of a male child is not the sole duty of the mother; all of the women in the harem participate. It is common practice for the women of the harem to pacify baby boys by fondling their genitals, and like extended breast-feeding this continues so long that

133

the child carries into adult life memories of women stroking his penis. Saudi boys come to believe very early in childhood that women are there to provide for their pleasure. Boys are constantly catered to, humored and generally kept happy by women both younger and older than they."[17]

Spied on by the Moral Police

Sandra Mackey further states, "When Saudi men teach their boys to have contempt for their mothers and the female world, without recognizing it, they are destroying the human race. Males and females emerge with their whole approach to life rooted in a warped outlook on sex and on each other. Sex is such a taboo that it is, ironically, the prime preoccupation of the Saudi culture.[18]

In centuries past, upper-class men crippled Chinese women's feet by binding them. The men's reason for this cruel act was to prevent uncivilized running around. The toes were twisted back under the instep and as the child's bones grew, formed a kind of fist, barely enabling them to walk as adults.

In early biblical times, men believed that if a woman became pregnant after rape that was a sign that she had derived pleasure from it.[19] If no conception took place, her moral virginity remained intact.

The History of Women, Volume II, also says, "Rape records of Episcopal courts in Northern France showed that young widows in particular were considered free game by young men of their villages. Gangs would set out at night, breaking into their houses, raping and mistreating them."[20] The book also mentioned their role in encouraging adultery by saying, "You can't often be with your lady, and it's hard for a young man to remain chaste. Why don't you try the maids?" The margrave Louis of Thuringia was teased in this fashion by his courtiers, we learn from his biography. Their remarks allude not only to their master's unlimited seigniorial rights over the female servants of his household, but also to his rights as a husband.[21]

When young men became aware that being male meant having access to certain sexual rites, including the right to buy a woman's body, it seemed it also gave them the right to take without consent—rape.

Rape in war was considered an act against the woman's husband and father, and considered the ultimate act of humiliation for the woman. Generally in war, it is the winning side that does the raping. So go the spoils of victory.

> For I am the Lord, your God, who takes hold of your right
> hand and says to you, Do not fear; I will help you.
> —Isaiah 41:13

CHAPTER 15

Dear Church

"Life isn't fair, but God is."

—L.R.S.

The church as a whole is ignorant, unprepared, and oblivious to the problem of sexual assault. Satan has taken advantage of the church's uninvolvement to continue to attack Christians and non-Christians alike.

"Additionally, the Christian community is almost wholly neglectful in teaching girls and women rape awareness and prevention. This gives church women a false sense of security and a harder time dealing with an actual assault. Some professionals feel that the number of persons in the Christian community who are victims of sexual abuse is extremely high because the church is naïve, thus vulnerable.

"The church produces a sad predicament for the victim of sexual violence. Most pastors say they rarely or never have had a rape victim come to them for counsel. Because sexual assault is so extensive, they agree it was not because a few church women were involved, but because the victim does not ask them for help. She senses, often correctly, that the collective church would respond to her with awkwardness and inappropriate assistance.

"Would churches then be receptive to a presentation to better understand the problem? A number of pastors say no. Because few victims have come forth, the clergy concludes it is not a concern within their congregation.

"Rape is a crime against God and humanity. The body of Christ is called to express God's love and healing to anyone experiencing grief and pain. Pastors and lay people need to recognize the rape victim as an individual who deserves their most compassionate and educated response. As salt of the earth, Christians have a unique opportunity and God-given responsibility to stem evil wherever it abounds. Apathy and ignorance give women the impression that sexual violence is the unmentionable sin."[1] (Candace Walters, Invisible Wounds)

While many pastors would like to help rape victims, they don't know how. Rape counseling is something most pastors do not learn in seminary. They agree it would be better to help survivors in the church family; however, few churches offer this service.

The church mistrusts secular rape counseling services. Likewise, rape crisis centers are skeptical of the ability of the church, as it has remained uninformed and uninvolved. Both secular and spiritual resources are beneficial. But if women are not given a spiritual choice in counseling, they may not seek help at all.

The church can encourage advocates to take training in rape awareness, prevention, and recovery. Then they can make the congregation aware that there are people ready to help. The church can provide a loving, nonjudgmental atmosphere as the survivor accepts answers to her pain and receives prayer for restoration—something she would not receive in a secular setting.

It's time to pray that the church will become involved in setting the rape captive free—free to be a vibrant survivor instead of a defeated victim.

Why Are Women Raped?

The most credible answer is that Satan is the instigator. An innocent person reaps the consequences of someone else's sinful choice. God allows such sinfulness because He has given every person a free will, and He doesn't stop people from choosing unrighteous acts.

The Bible teaches us that evil is always at war with good. God warned us in 1 Peter 5:8, "Your enemy the devil prowls around like a roaring lion looking for someone to devour."[2]

What Is Evil?

Evil resides in the heart of everyone. We walk a fine line between the heart of a harlot and that of a saint. When mankind chooses to do harm, either through thoughts, words, or acts, he commits evil. Evil is a behavior; it's always a matter of choice. Evil is inflicted.

"The heart is deceitful above all things and beyond cure."
—Jeremiah 17:9

Where Did Evil Come From?

". . . the great dragon . . . that ancient serpent called the devil, or Satan, who leads the whole world astray" (Rev. 12:9). He is referred to as "morning star, son of the dawn" in Isaiah 14:12. Morning star in Hebrew is translated as Lucifer in the Latin Vulgate. He is now known by many names: the devil, the dragon, the serpent, and Satan. He is a slanderer, devourer, deceiver, adversary and opponent. Satan induced man to sin.

Satan, the deceptive, insidious arch criminal, has kept people blind to his far-reaching effects. Mankind has been dulled to his hideous and horrific atrocities. We can only escape his influence and find safety in the arms of God.

When Did Evil Reveal Itself to Humankind?

Genesis in the Bible is called the book of origins. When God told Adam and Eve not to eat from the tree of the knowledge of good and evil, the serpent (Satan) tempted Eve. Both Adam and Eve ate of its fruit; thus sin entered in (Gen. 2:16-17).

Heaven wept when Eden fell victim to sin, filling the world with woe. All the hopes of men and angels were dashed. Nothing in the history of the world has ever come close to this calamity. All crimes and catastrophes may be traced to the original sin.

Every one of us is a free moral agent. We have the liberty to exercise power for good or evil. We could be tested in no other way. God could have made everyone perfect so that they could not do evil. If He had done that, we could not freely exercise our attributes. God would not have a reason to test and prove His people.

The heart is the foundation of affection and motive. It is that function which prompts action. If pollution enters the heart, pollution of action is almost certain to follow. "Keep thy heart with all diligence; for out of it are the issues of life" (Prov. 4:23 KJV).

PART 3
TAKING BACK CONTROL

RESTRUCTURING YOUR LIFE AFTER RAPE, AND GUIDANCE FOR THOSE WHO WANT TO HELP

"The soul can be damaged almost beyond repair."

—L.R.S.

Dear Reader

Because each one of us is unique, and we all perceive life differently, recovery from your sexual assault will find its own pace. Perhaps your wounds are ancient, but you have never fully recovered, and you are now ready to walk the healing path. Or your wound may be as fresh now as yesterday. Just reading and listening to things on the subject of rape may be challenging for you. That's okay. This workbook is meant to be used as a tool in your recovery, either alone or in a class setting; it is only a means to an end.

Rape is rape, whether it is committed by your father, uncle, brother, neighbor, or a stranger. While this book does not address incest in depth as a topic matter, it can be quite beneficial to incest survivors.

The purpose for women sharing their thoughts in a class-room setting is so they can learn how to be free of anger, bitterness, fear, and sorrow as a team. If you are studying alone, God is on the journey to wholeness with you. In any event, all of us walk a mutual path.

You have been damaged; your world has changed. But whether you get better or worse is up to you. Evil and its wreckage can be destroyed and God can create new life in you. As a group, others can take part in the birthing of your new life.

If you are working through the book by yourself, please be sure to complete all the writing assignments. They are powerful and will play a significant role in your recovery. Find a trusted friend or relative to share your writing with; they will be your confidant, encouraging you on.

If you continue turning these pages, I salute you—you are a woman of courage!

For those who want to help rape survivors recover, I salute you too. It takes as much courage to help others, as those who seek help.

Awesome blessings!

—Leila Rae

Gathered in Your Wings

I didn't know when it happened, this quiet calm
besieging me.
Gathered in Your wings of love, Your shadow hovered over.
My mind set free, my soul at peace.
I can't believe it's me.

—*L.R.S.*

NOTES

Some sections from Part I are repeated here in Part III. This is to reiterate and reinforce the subject matter for class discussion.

There are six sessions presented here. Each session can be studied in a separate weekly meeting. The schedules included in this chapter are for a typical evening meeting, from 6:00 to 9:00 P.M.

The class could also be taught in a three-day weekend. For example, Thursday evening for three hours, Friday evening for three hours, and Saturday for six to seven hours.

CHAPTER 16

Women in Recovery from Rape

SESSION I

Part One

6:00   Class orientation (Include some humor to break the ice.)

6:45   Share personal stories ("What do you want to gain from this class?")

7:05   Evaluation ("On a scale of one to ten, where are you in your recovery?")

7:20   Writing to heal

7:30   Break

Part Two

7:40   Introspection ("Who was I before the rape?")

7:45   Myths about rape

8:00   The three levels of victimization (level one: original trauma)

8:45   Taking care of you (Let God help)

8:55   Close

Prepare for Next Week: Bring humor to share.

Homework: Describe your sexual assault facts. Read session II.

Assignment: Write a "Dear God" letter.

Suggested Reading: *Writing to Be Whole* by Eddie Ensley and Robert Hermann

The night is far spent, the day is at hand: let us therefore cast off the works of darkness, and let us put on the armour of light.

—Romans 13:12 (KJV)

SESSION I

Part One

WRITING TO HEAL

"The longer we dwell on our misfortunes, the greater is their power to harm us."

—Voltaire

"Writing is a form of prayer that does something no other form of prayer can do: it makes visible the invisible. We have lots of mental clutter, and underneath that clutter are the images, memories, stories, and thoughts that form our spiritual core. In writing, we get a chance to see the clutter, deal with it, and then draw out these treasures from our core. Writing makes this inner world concrete. Our problems become visible. And when we see them clearly, we can then hand them over to the God who comforts and mends. Writing becomes dialogue with oneself. Writing helps the visionary part of us come to life again."[1]

The purpose of journaling is to process emotions. To process is to release. Putting our thoughts and feelings down on paper is an opportunity to be honest and open. Honor yourself by writing about your pain, loss and grief—then it will become a healing experience. Keeping your feelings locked up is damaging.

Louise De Salvo says in her book *Writing as a Way of Healing,* "Writing that describes traumatic or distressing events in detail and how we felt about these events then and feel about them now is the only kind of writing about trauma that clinically has been associated with improved health."[2]

NOTE: If you are suicidal, out of control, or feel you're still in a Post-Traumatic Stress Disorder high risk situation, seek professional help *immediately*. You don't want to retraumatize yourself. Revisiting trauma with your therapist/doctor is a safe place to write.

> Give sorrow words . . .
> —William Shakespeare

QUESTIONS TO ANSWER

Where Are You Now?

Describe your life right now.

_____

_____

_____

_____

_____

On a scale of one to ten—ten being the highest level of healing—where are you in your recovery?

_____

_____

_____

_____

_____

What happiness have you experienced this past year?

_____

_____

_____

_____

_____

What's bothering you the most right now?

_____

_____

_____

_____

_____

For You created my inmost being; You knit
me together in my mother's womb.
I praise You because I am fearfully and wonderfully made;
Your works are wonderful, I know that full well.
My frame was not hidden from You when I
was made in the secret place. When I was woven
together in the depths of the earth,
Your eyes saw my unformed body.
All the days ordained for me were written
in Your book before one of them came to be.
—Psalm 139:13-16

SESSION I

Part Two

WHO WERE YOU BEFORE THE RAPE?

As you move through the process of healing, you will forge a new self. The metaphor that works for me is of a crystal glass that is shattered, and then painstakingly put back together, piece by piece, with lead sutures holding the fragments. The original material is thus molded into a goblet of a much different design, strength, and beauty.[3]

If you were optimistic about yourself and the world before your rape, you may recover sooner than if life held unresolved problems, losses, former sexual abuse, and no support group. On the other hand, rape can come as more of a shock to a victim who has never encountered trauma than to one who has. A prior trauma experience can leave some survivors stronger; therefore, they are not damaged as severely.

Who were you before the rape? A little girl, a mother, housewife, career woman? What did your days hold? Did you play, garden, have hobbies, pursue outside interests, volunteer, or serve in the church or community?

What changed after your sexual assault? Did you withdraw, quit your job or volunteering, lose interest in hobbies, or isolate yourself?

Write down your answers:

_____

_____

_____

_____

_____

_____

_____

_____

_____

_____

_____

_____

_____

_____

_____

MYTHS AND FACTS ABOUT RAPE

One woman is raped somewhere in the United States every minute of every day. In the United States alone, FBI statistics show more than 100,000 women report being raped each year, and an estimated additional 400,000 to 900,000 are raped but do not report the crime. One in four women will be raped at some time in her life (*Recovery from Rape*, 1986, Linda E. Ledray).

Sex is used as a weapon to intimidate, control, and humiliate the rape victim. If rape was only motivated by sex,

Las Vegas would not have one of the highest rates of rape in the nation, even with legalized prostitution. However, police statistics prove they do.

Society sends confusing messages about sexual behavior. Many institutions and individuals tend to blame the victim for her rape. As a rape survivor, you need to examine and evaluate the extent to which you have accepted the victim-blaming attitudes of society.

Here are just a few examples of the myths surrounding rape:

- **Men rape for sexual release.**
- **Women enjoy or need a little rape.**
- **Only young, attractive women get raped.**
- **You didn't resist, so you must have wanted it.**
- **Date rape really isn't rape.**
- **Only cheap girls get raped.**
- **Men don't get raped.**

These are all myths. No mentally healthy woman wants to be raped. Men rape for power control. Babies, old women, Christians, and women of all faiths are raped. Women of all sizes, shapes, and looks are raped. Nice girls get raped. Men force sex on their dates. And yes, men do get raped.

It's time society quits treating rape and the degradation of women as a game. Myths about rape enable us to believe we live in a just world. We believe that if a woman dresses modestly, stays away from unsavory places, goes to church every Sunday, and minds her own business, she won't get raped. These claims give us a false sense of security, as they are pure fiction. More women are raped in their homes than any other place.

Rapists look like any average person. They are seldom mentally ill or deranged, and they often know or recognize their victims. Rape is a crime of violence and aggression, not a crime of passion. Rapists use sex as a weapon to degrade and terrorize women, to make them fear for their lives. As a result, the need to feel safe can become an addiction. "Did I lock the doors? Did I lock my car? Are the windows locked? I'd better go check again."

QUESTIONS TO ANSWER

Where were you raped?

_____

_____

_____

_____

Was your rapist a stranger or an acquaintance?

_____

_____

_____

_____

_____

THREE LEVELS OF VICTIMIZATION

Rape causes a crisis in a woman's life. It makes her feel overwhelmed, powerless, and out of control. All the familiar ways of managing and dealing with the world don't seem to work anymore.

Rape is probably the worst life crisis a woman will ever have to face. All components of a woman's self are violated in a sexual assault. Her property rights are trespassed; perhaps her home or car was illegally entered. Her personal possessions are plundered or used as weapons to tie, gag, blindfold, or hurt her. Her physical being is threatened, handled without consent, and usually injured. The most appalling and intimate violation, her inner self, is invaded. What greater insult can be committed by one human being against another?[4]

Victimization, which means the process of becoming a victim, can be considered to occur on three levels (McCarthy 1986).[5] In brief, the levels are:

- **Level One: The original trauma (such as sexual assault)**
- **Level Two: Secondary wounding (such as your loved ones not believing you)**
- **Level Three: Society's view of the trauma**

Describe your original trauma, your secondary wounding, and how you think society views rape.

_____

_____

_____

_____

_____

_____

_____

_____

_____

_____

_____

_____

_____

_____

_____

LEVEL-ONE VICTIMIZATION: ORIGINAL TRAUMA

"Help! What's happening to me?"

Shock

You have experienced trauma, and you are (or were) in shock as a result. Your system went into overload in order to deal with your new reality. This happens to everyone encountering trauma, especially rape. Our bodies and minds make up the whole of our being. When trauma hits us, like an earthquake, our bodies and minds rattle, making us temporarily disjointed. Shock is the immediate aftermath that leaves you emotionally and physically numb, confused, and in a state of hyper-arousal.

The effects of shock can cause you to think you remembered your trauma wrong, minimizing it—maybe it wasn't as bad as you thought. After a trauma such as rape, you tend to think differently; your memory, emotions, and perceptions are not the same as before.

Hyper-arousal occurs because, when the trauma hit, you went on full alert. Oddly, well after the trauma is over, you remain on full alert. The switch that was turned on doesn't turn off, maintaining a state of hyper-arousal. The effects are trouble sleeping, difficulty concentrating, heightened vigilance, being easily startled, feeling wary, sudden crying, unexpected anger, deeper emotions, panicking, intensified alertness, increased anxiety, and reminders of the trauma. This leads to physical reactions such as rapid heart beat and sweating.[6]

Denial and Disbelief

These reactions typically occur after the initial impact of the trauma.

Denial refuses to believe that something exists. Some denial can help with feelings of helplessness, abandonment, the fear of the perpetrator returning, and the fear of death. Denial can be your friend immediately after a trauma. Temporary denial, in small doses, protects you and allows you to cope.

When the shock of emotional wounding has occurred, denial is necessary. The overwhelming impact of rape needs the softening, anesthetic balm of denial. Denial distracts our minds so we can recover at our own pace. Our trauma tells our minds to refuse the reality of our rape; it's too painful to face.

God carries us in the palm of His hands during this time. "For in the time of trouble, He shall hide me in His pavilion" (Ps. 27:5 KJV). Shock and denial will pass in time; then we can accept what occurred and move forward.

Disbelief is, by far, the overriding effect on your thinking. At first, you cannot make your thoughts believe what has happened to you. Like denial, disbelief is protective. It keeps you from believing your thoughts, which are, at the moment, incomprehensible. There is no preparation for such shocking, sudden events.

Because you couldn't think about this event ahead of time there is not a place in your thoughts for it. A place has to be created in your thoughts *after* the trauma.[7]

Rage and Anger

These are normal reactions after being raped. Anger at the rapist, anger that the assault took place, anger at the disruption of your life, anger at those close to you. The slightest thing can cause anger to erupt. "Now, where did that come from?" you may ask after blowing up. It scares you because you suddenly feel out of control.

In time, this abrupt rage and anger will cease. Be patient. And remember, these episodes won't last forever. Seek counseling if your anger and rage continue.

Depression

When a person has been subjected to severe stress, such as rape, the biological neurotransmitter system is disturbed. This system becomes so strained it cannot perform its functions as it did before the traumatic event. This physiological breakdown can lead to negative thinking, lack of concentration, low self-esteem, hopelessness, difficulty in decision-making, and sleep disorders. Other classic symptoms of depression are irritability, anxiety, loss of pleasure with others and activities, and sensitivity to the reactions of others.

Depression often grabs hold of a traumatized person, and it doesn't always happen immediately. It can surface much later, after the trauma has occurred. With so many issues to address after sexual assault, depression is often camouflaged. When we are left with the feeling of loss (losing our old self, loss of a reliable world, loss of safety, etc.), depression can take over. Depression can also trigger losses or a bad attitude from the past, compounding our out-of-control condition.

Depression can leave us feeling sad, powerless, helpless, fatigued, lethargic, down on ourselves, uninterested in life, or suicidal. However, depression usually passes when our normal way of living has been resumed, mourning is completed, and steps to resolution are taken (such as rape recovery classes or counseling).

If your depression persists, see your doctor. Have him give you a physical and see if he thinks anti-depressants should be prescribed. Extended counseling may also be beneficial.

Plea Bargaining

Sometimes a rape survivor tries to bargain with God. "If you make the pain go away, I'll never commit that recurring sin of mine again." This kind of bargaining makes the survivor believe she is guilty, and that is unhealthy thinking.

QUESTIONS TO ANSWER

1. Name your anger. Identify one or more persons you are angry at right now.
2. What kind of denying or bargaining, if any, have you made?

MY PRAYER

God of Mercy,
Pierce my daunting spirit. Make me a poster child for Your grace. Shine bright on my soul. Exchange my heart of stone for a heart of flesh. Help me to love as You love, and to forgive as You have forgiven, that I might stand, someday, in glory before You. Amen.

—L.R.S.

WRITING TO GOD

If you want healing for your soul, eventually you will have to look at your deepest fears, express your most keenly felt regrets, and describe your losses. But this healing journey is not along a lonely pathway or through a solitary valley. Walking beside you will be the One who dries your tears and warms your heart with a comfort that flows from eternity. You will find safety when you meet the God of all comfort.

You cannot manufacture God's comfort, for it is free. It is a gift. But while you cannot generate comfort, you can ask for it. You can say yes to it, and you can make space in your heart for it. Jesus spoke of this safety, this peace that abides in the mystery of the brightness of God, when He said, "Peace I leave with you; My peace I give to you. I do not give to you as the world gives" (John 14:27).[8]

Christians are not immune from the misfortunes of life, including sexual violence. Rape, along with life's other tragedies, can happen to anyone. The providence of God does not always spare Christians from life's adversities. Suffering is a universal experience borne by both the godly and the wicked. The Bible doesn't say that nothing bad will ever happen to us. But it does say, in Romans 8:35-39, that nothing that does happen to us can ever separate us from the love of God.[9]

Assignment: Write a letter or poem to God and tell Him about your hurt and pain.

_____

_____

_____

_____

_____

_____

_____

_____

_____

_____

_____

_____

_____

_____

_____

_____

_____

_____

_____

_____

_____

_____

_____

_____

_____

_____

ONE WOMAN'S LETTER

Dear God,

I hurt because of the things I've written about. I hurt because I find that I can't say no when I want to. I can't say how I really feel much of the time. I have depression and anxiety problems. I have trouble handling money and I have problems overeating. I have trouble taking good care of myself. I have trouble setting goals, having fun, and feeling joy.

I need Your help to heal whatever has given all these things such a firm hold on me. Help me, please, to heal. There's a lot I don't remember. A lot I don't know for sure. Some things I'm afraid of. I need Your help!

I thank You for what You've done in my life, for the healing You're doing now. I thank You for Your love and mercy and for salvation.

—Jane

MY LETTER TO GOD

Dear Heavenly Father God,
I come to You with all that I am. I stand unveiled before You, asking for restoration. Only You know the depth of my pain; only You can heal the sorrows of my past. Gather me with tenderness under Your wings. Shed light upon my face so that I might feel the warmth of Your mercies. Let me feel Your presence that I might find new strength. Quiet my soul so I might hear Your still, small voice. Whisper Your eternal message of love. Guide me toward new pathways that lead to joy, healing, and forgiveness. Amen.

—L. R. S.

EVIL RESIDES IN THE HEART OF EVERYONE

We walk a fine line between the heart of a harlot and that of a saint. When mankind chooses to do harm, either through thoughts, words, or acts, he commits evil. Evil is a behavior; it is always a matter of choice. Evil is inflicted. "The heart is deceitful above all things and beyond cure" (Jer. 17:9).

Evil started with Satan, and it is he who instigates it. "Your enemy the devil prowls around like a roaring lion looking for someone to devour" (1 Pet. 5:8).

Everyone is a free moral agent. We have the liberty to exercise power for good or evil. We could be tested in no other way. God could have made everyone perfect so they could not do evil. If He had done that, we could not freely exercise our attributes, thus making it unnecessary for God to test and prove His people.

The heart is the foundation of affection and motive. If pollution enters the heart, pollution of action is almost certain to follow. "Keep thy heart with all diligence; for out of it are the issues of life" (Prov. 4:23 KJV).

TAKE GOOD CARE OF
YOURSELF—YOU DESERVE IT

Here are some examples of be-good-to-yourself comforts:

- **Plenty of rest and exercise**
- **Get back to a scheduled routine**
- **Seek rape/post-traumatic counseling**
- **Get a current physical**
- **Do something fun that you enjoy**
- **Seek a support group, someone to confide in, or both.**

What personal comforts can you add to this list? Choose one that you promise to do for yourself this week.

COPING

Do some silly things to relieve tension, fear, and worry. You could roll down a grassy slope, kiss a puppy, jump up and down in rain puddles (preferably with the neighbor kids), play hopscotch or jump rope. Study the insects in your garden—your potted plants if you don't have a garden. Amaze yourself by lightening up.

**YOU ARE AWESOME,
O' WOMAN OF COURAGE!**

CHAPTER 17

Women in Recovery from Rape

SESSION II

Part One

6:00 Share humor, read letters to God, share rape experience facts

6:50 Post-Traumatic Stress

7:10 Triggers

7:30 Break

Part Two

8:00 The three levels of victimization (level two: victimization/secondary wounding)

8:30 Taking care of yourself ("Where's God?"); stimuli (before, during, after rape)

8:55 Close

Prepare for Next Week: Bring humor to share.

Homework: Bring stimuli facts about your rape. Read Session III.

Assignment: Write letter *to* you *from* God.

Suggested Reading: *The Wounded Heart* by Dr. Dan Allender (for adult survivors of childhood sexual abuse).

Be not be overcome by evil, but overcome evil with good.

—Romans 12:21

SESSION II

Part One

POST-TRAUMATIC STRESS

"Post-Traumatic Stress has been called a sane reaction to an insane situation."[1]

Everyone faces crises sometime during their life. The crisis can be as small as losing your car keys to as powerful as the loss of a loved one. These crises are stressful, but not traumatic. Traumatic events refer to situations in which great danger is involved. You are powerless and helpless, and the trauma horrific. These are not the normal, everyday events.

The magnitude of such events overtaxes one's ability to cope. Everyone confronts the facts of mortality. However, the reality of death confronts rape survivors more vividly than most.

Benjamin Colodzin, Ph.D., says in his book *How to Survive Trauma*, "I do not like to use the term 'Post-Traumatic Stress Disorder' since it is not always useful to think of this pattern of functioning as a medical disorder. Therefore, I will drop the D for disorder." He goes on to say, "It makes it easier to concentrate on the person who has lived through something overwhelming rather than on symptoms of a disease. So, we will refer to PTSD as Post-Traumatic Stress."[1]

One experience of rape in the life of an adult changes the color of that person's world forever. Once any trauma has occurred, the illusion that the world is safe is destroyed. Gone forever.[2]

Some symptoms of traumatic stress have been covered earlier, such as rage/anger, depression, shock, denial, and disbelief. Now we'll add some new ones to the list.

Hyper-Alert Response: Constant vigilance and scanning; always looking around as though something dangerous is about to happen.

Hyper-Startle Response: Being jumpy, edgy, easily startled.

Memory and Concentration Interrupted: Memory recall can be short; you may have difficulty concentrating.

Anxiety: The physical body tenses, leading to stomach-aches, headaches, back pain, and the mind carrying worried thoughts like unfounded fears, terror, and fear of death.

Panic: Panic is feeling like you are coming apart inside. It is associated with the fear that you will be harmed (raped) again. You feel out of control and unable to cope. Being alone, remembering your brush with death, knowing this is an unsafe world, and hearing, seeing, or smelling something that reminds you of the event can bring on a panic attack.

Mood Swings: Mood swings can happen any time, any day. You can feel great one minute, then awful the next.

Psychic Numbing: An inability to experience love, playfulness, joy, or bonding with other people.

Can you name other side effects of rape?

_____

_____

_____

_____

_____

What were your symptoms of Post-Traumatic Stress? Do you still experience them?

_____

_____

_____

_____

_____

_____

_____

COPING WITH TRIGGERS

A triggering event is when something happens in the present moment, often unexpectedly, that in some way reminds you of what happened then. Under certain conditions, noises, smells, sights, thoughts, or feelings that are associated with what happened can act as triggers.[3] This is called stimuli.

A trigger situation is threatening because, consciously or unconsciously, you feel powerless and vulnerable to attack. Old memories surface, bringing painful thoughts of anger, fear, and grief. Triggers can make you feel out of control. You think you are going crazy. The thought that you are mentally ill is terrifying. Feeling safe is a major priority in the life of a rape survivor.

When you know your triggers are linked to the past and have nothing to do with the present, your feelings are more manageable. Differentiating the past from the present will make the present feel safer.

TRIGGER CHART EXAMPLES

Trigger	My Reaction	Traumatic Memory
Someone talks gruffly or scowls	Fear, repulsion	Perpetrator ordered me to remove my clothes
White sleeveless blouses	Anxiety	I wore a white sleeveless blouse the night of rape
Lights go off at night	Pounding heart, sweating, panic	Electricity was cut the night of the rape

QUESTIONS TO ANSWER

What triggers have you experienced?

_____

_____

_____

_____

_____

Then . . .

_____

_____

_____

_____

_____

Now...

_____

_____

_____

_____

_____

If your sexual assault was decades ago, do you still have trigger points? If so, what are they?

_____

_____

_____

_____

_____

_____

_____

_____

_____

_____

_____

_____

_____

SESSION II

Part Two

LEVEL-TWO VICTIMIZATION: SECONDARY WOUNDING

A secondary wound happens when people say things, intentionally or unintentionally, that deepen your already wounded soul. Secondary wounding is often as painful as shooting a bullet into your heart. It is as deadly as the original traumatic event. Healing from your secondary wounding is every bit as important as healing from your original assault.

Here are some examples of accusing remarks that can heap guilt on survivors:

- **"If you'd learned how to use a gun, the assault might not have happened."**
- **"Why were you there in the first place?"**
- **"I'm sorry you were raped, but we have to continue our own ministries."**

Because of the biological changes that can occur after a rape, victims become exceptionally sensitive to other people's responses. Secondary wounding from others will affect you more than a non-traumatized person. Learn to distance yourself from negative people.

It isn't easy countering the powerful negative messages of secondary wounding, and they will probably always trouble you at times. But, as you make progress in finding self-worth and value, you will feel less a victim and more a survivor.

SECONDARY WOUNDING RESPONSES

There are many types of secondary wounding, from blaming the survivor for his/her problems, exhibiting ignorance, labeling, and just plain cruelty. Being able to identify the responses of others will increase your ability to cope in a constructive manner. Of course the pain and humiliation will still be present, but naming these responses can lessen your secondary wounding.

Here Are a Few Categories:

Discounting: Many times people discount the fact that your rape took place, or they minimize it by saying, "It could have been worse. You could have been killed." Remarks like these make one feel guilty, ungrateful, and embarrassed that they even told their story.

Denial and Disbelief: When people say things like, "Oh, come on, that couldn't really have happened," they are not accepting the reality of your trauma.

Blaming the Survivor: Some people talk as though the victim were to blame, at least in part, for what happened. "You probably shouldn't have been there after dark. Maybe it was the dress you were wearing. What about that drink you had?"

Generalization: One of the social consequences of being traumatized is that the public tends to label you as a victim. People interpret your behavior and emotions in light of that label. For example, "You poor thing."

Trauma Ignorance: Many people have never experienced trauma; therefore, they do not know what to say or do. Some people are fearful when they hear of your rape. It reminds them of their vulnerability to victimization. Some people rattle on, making you feel insignificant and small.

Cruelty: Secondary wounding almost always feels cruel, even if the other person isn't aware that his words are demeaning. Someone hearing of your rape may try to make light of it by telling a rape joke or saying, "Yeah, tell me about it," as if your trauma was a normal occurrence common to everyone. Our culture has become increasingly emotionally detached, even within the family. Economic and social changes make it difficult for people to empathize with one another.

QUESTIONS TO ANSWER

What about you? Has someone made hurtful remarks like these to you? What were they? How did they make you feel?

_____

_____

_____

_____

_____

What is your secondary wounding attitude today? Has your attitude changed toward society, church, or types/groups of people? Has your attitude changed toward family, friends, or others? Has your attitude affected your ability to participate in clubs, associations, and public activities? Explain your secondary wounding attitude after your rape, what it is like now, and how you plan to overcome secondary wounding.

_____

_____

_____

_____

_____

_____

_____

_____

_____

_____

_____

_____

_____

_____

_____

_____

_____

_____

_____

TAKING CARE OF YOURSELF

Being raped is a crisis. Crises create stress—in your personal life, in other people's lives, and in your relationships. Stress is difficult to manage. There are, however, some techniques you can use to help lessen the tension and bring some ease into your life. A good first step is to remember what tactics have worked for you in the past in coping with difficult periods in your life.[4]

Try these be-good-to-yourself comforts:

- **Go to the library.** Silence can be calming. The sights and smells of old books, like old friends, are comforting.
- **Work in the garden.** Puttering in the garden slows you down and allows your mind to rest.
- **Visit garden nurseries.** Strolling in a garden center (if you like gardening) commands your mind to pay attention to plants, eliminating disturbing thoughts.
- **Visit a favorite coffee house.** Hands wrapped around a warm, yummy hot drink in the winter or a cold, icy drink in the summer is soothing. It's better than wrapping your hands around someone's neck (in anger)! Sipping a drink and people-watching is relaxing.
- **A soaking bath.** A hot or cold (depending on the season) bubble bath can do wonders for your attitude.
- **Learn a new pastime.** Try some hand work such as knitting, crochet, needlepoint, embroidery, weaving, quilting, or rug hooking. Maybe try floral design, calligraphy, writing, painting, doll making, cake decorating, or learning to play a musical instrument.
- **Befriend an elderly person.** Let wisdom, knowledge, and wonder seep into you from her. Volunteer to write

letters or run errands for her. Bake cookies together. Buy her a cute pair of jeans—it will make her feel young.

- **Take back control.** Once you've cried over your assault memory again and again until there are no more tears, start focusing on how far you have come. Remind yourself that you cheated death, you are alive, and you will recover.
- **Tour your own home town.** Discover what others come to see.
- **Read comic books.** Only the funny ones.
- **Read the Bible.** And count your blessings.

QUESTIONS TO ANSWER

What comforting activities can you add to the list?

_____

_____

_____

_____

_____

What comfort did you give yourself last week?

_____

_____

_____

_____

Pick a new comfort for yourself for next week.

_____

_____

_____

_____

WHERE'S GOD?

> Be not overcome of evil, but overcome evil with good.
> —Romans 12:21 (KJV)

Many Christian women assume they have divine protection from sexual assault. Rape was never discussed at their churches, which leads them to believe only unbelievers or backsliders are assaulted. When a Christian woman is raped, she may wonder if God is punishing her. Her friends and family may wonder if it came upon her due to past sins. A sexual assault can leave a woman's faith shattered.

"A Christian victim must overcome an additional obstacle: many people stifle the efforts of an individual believer to express any negative thoughts or feelings. This is particularly damaging to a survivor of rape. Not many understand how she truly feels. They discount the seriousness of her assault. She may be urged to praise God when she feels abandoned by Him. She may be offered Bible verses and platitudes which sound cruel and superficial to her. She may be pressured to carry on as if everything is normal when, in fact, her world has fallen apart."[5]

Try not to make your sexual assault a permanent disability. All of us will face suffering in this life, but God can bring hope and restoration into the worst circumstances. He is able to turn evil into good (Gen. 50:20). We can find meaning in our pain; our sorrow will not be wasted. Human nature sees nothing redemptive in our trauma, but God can use our afflictions to draw us close to Him and reveal awesomeness to an unbelieving world.

"Where is God when bad things happen?" you ask. When tragedy invades our lives, without purpose or explanation, we tend to wonder why God allowed it. We sometimes believe God doesn't care about us. But God is a loving, righteous God. The character of God is kind, perfect, holy, and always does what is good and right. We will not always have the answer to "why?" However, we can be assured of His compassion. He will lead us out of the darkness of sorrow into the light of acceptance.

Last week, you wrote a letter to God expressing your pain and hurt. If you wanted to receive a letter *from* Him, consoling you, what would you want it to say? Listen for that still, small voice whispering to your soul.

Assignment: Write such a letter to yourself from God.

_____

_____

_____

_____

_____

_____

_____

_____

_____

_____

_____

_____

_____

_____

_____

_____

_____

_____

_____

_____

_____

_____

_____

_____

_____

_____

_____

_____

_____

ONE WOMAN'S LETTER

My child,

I have waited for you. You have no idea how precious you are to Me. I've been with you all along, hurting when you hurt, wanting to offer comfort, and rejoicing when you have rejoiced, even if for wrong reasons.

You are one whom I have created, and I've been wanting to raise you up in all the glories I have for you. I know it is difficult to understand, but try to participate in this truth. I love you so much that I will not violate your essence by taking away your will or forcing My ways on you. I have respected the choices of man, releasing him to his choices for a set season. All offenses will one day be set right.

I do not wish for any of My children to hurt. Yet I am Justice and I am Mercy. I am big enough to allow time for repentance for the offender, as well as to heal and comfort the offended. I have not left either without what they need.

All you will ever need is here if you will just believe I have it for you and ask. I will not force anything upon you, as man forces his will on you. I love you.

I am pleased with My creation and I will move heaven and earth to reestablish you to health, wholeness, peace, joy and serenity. Look to Me; let Me show you the master copy of your existence. You will see the beauty I see. Let Me love you and heal your wounds. I love you, My child—I do . . . God

—Ann

STIMULI TRIGGERS

After a woman has been raped, she can respond to certain situations and everyday activities and stimuli in ways that seem peculiar. These strange reactions can be triggered by stimuli connected to you before, during, and after your rape. Recognizing these stimuli triggers will help you understand your reactions, leaving you less troubled by their occurrences.

For example, if your rapist told you to remove your clothes, then later, a nurse said, "Remove your clothes," hearing those words could trigger a negative reaction.

What specific sounds, smells, tastes, colors, words, objects, or gestures do you remember before, during, and after your rape?

O' little one, it is I who wept when evil came your way. I hung your pain around My neck and nailed it to the cross.

—L.R.S.

YOU ARE AMAZING,
O' WOMAN OF COURAGE!

CHAPTER 18

Women in Recovery from Rape

SESSION III

Part One

6:00 Humor, read letters from God, share stimuli facts
6:45 Fear
7:20 Biological changes
7:50 Break

Part Two

8:00 Reconstructing your life
8:40 Taking care of yourself ("It's me again, God")
8:55 Close

Prepare for next week: Bring humor to share.
Homework: Read Session IV.
Assignment: Write down the stimuli that trigger reactions for you.
Suggested reading: *I Can't Get Over It* by Aphrodite Matsakis (a rape recovery book).

I will bring health and healing to [her]; I will heal [her] and will let [her] enjoy abundant peace and security.
—Jeremiah 33:6

SESSION III

Part One

FEAR

The most widespread fear that rape survivors experience is the fear of death. It is the dominant emotional consequence of rape. Most survivors did not expect to live through the rape.

Rape victims are left fearful in their homes and communities. They are left with anxiety, nightmares, insomnia, addiction to tranquilizers, health problems, and fatigue.

Traumatic events are things that happen outside usual experiences, events that are so intensely frightening, painful, and threatening that they have overwhelmed our ability to feel secure about our place in the world. If you continue to feel overwhelmed by something traumatic that has happened in your life, the path to healing includes learning to become aware of, and be honest about, what frightened you so strongly that it damaged your sense of security.[1]

The human nervous system, which includes the brain and all the various networks of nerves, is our central computer system for processing information about what is happening inside and outside the body. This computer sends commands to the rest of the body, telling all the parts how to act in line with the information it has gathered about current conditions.

One type of command sent through the nervous system is a built-in one that is activated on "automatic pilot" whenever we perceive the conditions around us to be sufficiently threatening. This command is known as the "fight or flight" reflex. It switches on when certain conditions tell us that threat is nearby; that is, when we are frightened. When this command is received, a series of electrochemical events takes place within our bodies that affects heart rate, breathing, muscle tension levels, various chemical fluid balances, and a lot more.

All these reactions taken together comprise the "fight or flight" reflex. This reflex is built into the nervous system in order to alert our bodies quickly and help us survive the danger. However, this reflex cannot distinguish between real and imaginary danger. Every time we believe there is something threatening us, even if we are interpreting the situation incorrectly, the "fight or flight" reflex produces a jolt of energy.[2]

Fear resulting from rape is true fear. It is equivalent to seeing a train racing toward you, or your plane about to go down, or someone trying to break into your home. However, unfounded fear is also crippling. Worry (which is unfounded fear) is not true fear. Worry is anticipating that something awful is going to happen. Since I'm worried that the elevator will get stuck, the ship will go down, or the horse will fall, I refuse to enter an elevator, go on a cruise, or ride a horse.

When something appears threatening, a trauma survivor does not only see what's going on in the present, but the mind remembers previous assaults from the past, blurring the ability to distinguish between what is real and what is not.

Ask yourself, "Is this a question of my survival?" If your answer is no, your "fight or flight" reflex intensity will be reduced, and your pounding heart will calm down.

It isn't so much that you fear another assault. It's not knowing what the future holds.

It's the unpredictable that scares us. Fear is the most crippling disease known to mankind.

It can be the driving force in our perception of life.

We cannot eliminate the causes of fear, but we don't have to let them control our lives. Trust God for the future—He's already there.

It's normal for a woman who has been raped to be fearful. Do whatever it takes to feel safe. You may want to stay a short time with a friend or family member. Eventually, those scary feelings will pass. Everyone recovers at their own pace. It may be weeks, months, or years. However, if fear and pain linger too long, you should seek professional counseling to resolve it.

QUESTIONS TO ANSWER

What was your greatest fear during the rape? Were children or loved ones present at the time? Did the perpetrator make threats? Did he act erratically, adding more danger to your assault?

_____

_____

_____

_____

_____

What is your greatest fear now? If the criminal got away, do you fear his return? If he is soon to be released from jail, do you fear he might try to find you and retaliate?

_____

_____

_____

_____

_____

BIOLOGICAL CHANGES

Sexual assault can be as traumatizing to your psyche as to your body. The wounding of your spirit and emotions can affect your will to live. The assault changes the way you view the world and your sense of safety. The way you handled stress in the past is no longer adequate.

Because the memory tract in our brains can be altered by trauma, biological changes take place. Certain objects, situations, people, or smells can trigger re-experiencing your assault. Even when friends, counselors, and family members tell you that you are safe, you feel the same as when you were experiencing your assault. Biochemically your body screams, "Help! He's still here! Can't you see him?"

Even if your central nervous system has been affected, you can minimize many of these negative effects by learning new coping techniques, such as those mentioned in this book.

Assignment: List some ways you can self-talk to calm your psyche.

_____

_____

_____

_____

_____

_____

_____

_____

_____

_____

_____

_____

_____

_____

_____

_____

_____

_____

_____

_____

_____

_____

_____

_____

_____

_____

_____

_____

_____

SESSION III

Part Two

RECONSTRUCTING YOUR LIFE

Rape changes your perception of life. What once seemed important may hold little value now. When something as traumatic as rape occurs, survivors are given the opportunity to make positive changes in their lives. While this can be challenging, it is possible.

Fear, anger and grief need not have a stronghold on your life. You can take back control. With good counseling, friends, support groups, and sound coping strategies, you can begin the process of reconstructing your life.

Your willingness to change is apparent by the fact that you are reading this book. Having a positive view of yourself is helpful in the reconstructing process.

Learn to take control of runaway thoughts that dominate your mind. When intrusive thoughts of your rape flood your mind, stop and say, "It's all over. I'm safe now. He is nowhere near." As you reconstruct your life, fear, anger, self-blame, and the blame of others will have less control over you.

As we move through the process of healing, we forge a new self. The metaphor that works for me is of a crystal glass that is shattered, and then painstakingly put back together, piece by piece, with lead sutures holding the fragments. The original material is thus molded into a goblet of a much different design, strength, and beauty.[3]

QUESTIONS TO ANSWER

What is the positive side to your rape?

You are probably stunned by such a question, but out of every trial comes enrichment. We need to transform our negativity into reclaiming some of what was lost by discovering what we have gained; for example: compassion for others, re-evaluation of goals and values, strength you didn't know you had. List new discoveries about yourself; describe what you have gained in place of your loss.

Positive Things I Have Gained Since I Was Raped

- A closer relationship with God
- Compassion for others
- Diminished value for some things in my life; a greater value for others
- I cherish life more abundantly
- I have a greater appreciation for God's beautiful world
- My writing has gained strength
- I have a new appreciation for men (Yes, I know that sounds strange!)
- I have gotten rid of a lot of my old bad attitudes

TAKING CARE OF YOURSELF

Don't Blame Yourself

Many women feel as if they should have done something to avoid being raped. If you could have done something to avoid it, you would have. Believe me, no woman wants to be raped, and to insinuate otherwise is insane. Remember, the rapist is the one who committed the crime, not you.

Don't take the rap for the rapist. And don't let others blame you. They were not there. And it could just as well have happened to them.

Here are some more be-good-to-yourself comforts:

- **Treat yourself as someone important.** You are important, and you deserve to treat yourself as such. Do something special, something you've always wanted to do.

- **Indulge at your favorite restaurant.** Enjoy your favorite food—in moderation.

- **Flowers.** If you don't have a flower garden, purchase flowers for your office and/or your home. Put them by your bed, in your bathroom, on the kitchen counter, and by your cozy chair.

- **Bake Bread.** Nothing beats the smell of fresh-baked bread. Making it by hand is relaxing as you kneed it. Tasting the first bite is pure heaven. Okay, so you're on a diet. Reward yourself with a small piece, and give the rest away or put it in your freezer for visitors.

- **Take a snooze.** Give yourself permission to take a nap. Napping should be a national pastime. A nap restores and refreshes the soul, mind, and body, and it's free! Don't feel guilty when you lie down; your body is telling you to. The hour you think you have lost will be replaced with a revived spirit and new energy. A good nap helps remove stress and restores a healthy attitude. So snooze—zzz.

- **Get involved socially.** Increased social activities and social contact provide you with outlets to come against intrusive thoughts of your assault. Volunteer. If you are busy doing something for someone else, there won't be time to dwell on yourself.

- **Quick fixes.** These include walking (with or without your dog), relaxation exercises, physical exercise (like roller skating), and positive self-talk.
- **Deep breathing exercises.** The increased oxygen flow to your brain that results from a good calming exercise will increase your ability to think clearly, help with concentration, and rid the body of many toxins. Try this: Breathing deeply from your abdomen, inhale slowly to the count of five. Pause and hold your breath to the count of five. Exhale slowly to the count of five. Say the word relax three or four times, then repeat the exercise. Do this exercise smoothly and regularly for five minutes.
- **Give yourself affirmative pep talks.** Continue to tell yourself the rape was not your fault, that you are not afraid, and that you will be victorious.

IT'S ME AGAIN, GOD

Candace Walters says, in her book *Invisible Wounds*, "Remember that you are wounded, not dead. And for every wound there is a healing process. Many women think they'll never recover from rape. While it's natural to feel that way, it is another means Satan uses to further destroy a victim's life. When you consider your wound to be fatal, you may then neglect the many resources available to heal victims of sexual violence, including a God who proved new life could come out of the worst suffering. There will be many miserable moments when you might feel as if your sanity and life have been permanently destroyed. Those feelings come and go. You may misinterpret or overreact to comments made by others that are meant to be helpful. Bible verses that once were comforting and positive may now seem offensive and negative.

"There is the tendency to think that rape is the one insurmountable problem outside of God's intervention. While rape is probably man's foulest outrage against a fellow human being, there is no situation where God is not involved and concerned. God hates all evil, especially rape. When His children suffer, He also suffers. However disgusting or shattering your circumstance, God has the power to repair and restore."[4]

I am the Lord, who heals you.

—Exodus 15:26

YOU ARE INCREDIBLE,
O' WOMAN OF COURAGE!

CHAPTER 19

Women in Recovery from Rape

Session IV

Part One

6:00   Prayer and humor
6:45   Safety/assertiveness
7:15   Finding balance
7:50   Break

Part Two

8:00   The three levels of victimization (level three: society's view)
8:40   Taking care of yourself ("What about God?")
8:55   Close

Prepare for Next Week: Bring humor to share.

Homework: Indulge in a be-good-to-yourself comfort. Read Session V.

Assignment: Write a letter to your rapist and others who have wounded you.

Suggested Reading: *Recovery From Rape* by Linda Ledray

Forget the former things; do not dwell on the past. See, I am doing a new thing! Now it springs up; do you not perceive it?

—Isaiah 43:18-19

SESSION IV

Part One

SAFETY AND ASSERTIVENESS

The healing process begins by feeling safe. You can begin to feel safe by changing your thoughts and behaviors. How you will establish a sense of safety depends on the nature of your trauma. You are the only one who knows what will make you feel safe.

Empowerment begins by taking care of yourself physically and emotionally. Your traumatic experience left you feeling helpless in the face of danger. Feeling safe and secure is now your prime goal. Feeling safe will leave you comfortable with your emotions.

Establishing safety for your home might include improved locks for doors and windows, securing basement windows, removing overgrown shrubs near windows and doors, outdoor security lighting, installing a security system, or having a cell phone by your bed. Leave a couple of night lights on inside, and leave porch lights on or install censor lights that come on automatically.

Other safety precautions may include carrying a cell phone, parking as close to buildings as possible, asking a fellow employee to walk you to your car after work when it is dark.

Always maintain your car in good running order, avoid parking in dark, out-of-the-way places, and make sure your car always has at least a half tank of gas. Carry a "Help! Call police!" banner in your car. Take a self-defense class.

Assignment: Name additional safety precautions you can take.

Assertiveness Training Exercise

This exercise has proven helpful to trauma survivors. It will immediately leave you feeling empowered.

The class divides in half, with everyone facing one another. The object is to walk toward each other, one couple at a time, and pass, walking tall, shoulders back, head held erect, with relaxed, loose hands.

This exercise is especially important to rape survivors. It will give you a sense of confidence and control. Your assertive posture tells others, "Don't get any silly ideas—you may get more than you bargained for!"

Do this with a friend if you aren't in a class setting.

Balancing Exercise

You need to seek balance in order to efficiently function in the tasks you have chosen to perform. When you are balanced, you have planted your feet in such a way that what happens in your life cannot knock you off balance very easily. One of the best ways to learn about balance is by doing it.[1]

Many cultures have their own variations of an exercise called Pushing Hands. I learned about this exercise in a mental health class in college, and then discovered it again in the book *How to Survive Trauma* by Benjamin Colodzin, Ph.D.

It goes like this: Two people stand and face each other, two or three feet apart, legs spread slightly, toes pointed forward. Place your arms in front of you, palms forward and fingers raised, lined up with the other player's hands. You may lean forward on your toes or backward on your heels, but you may not move your foot position. If you move your foot position, this is defined as losing your balance (and the game).

You may make contact only with the hands of the other player. You may push as hard as you want. The object is not to make yourself the victor and the other person the loser, but simply to avoid losing your balance. Winning is defined as the ability to push outward with your force and to receive the force of the other player without moving your foot position.[2]

You can easily lose your physical balance because of mental or emotional imbalances that come up while you are engaged in playing the game. This game makes you aware that it's sometimes necessary to bend in order to maintain your balance. Push Hands begins to make you aware of your own particular style of projecting and receiving force, a style that you may use all your life. Further, it provides opportunities to learn how to handle force in a balanced manner. Force is "excessive" when its use causes you to lose your balance. Balance is using an efficient amount of energy to achieve your goals.[3]

SESSION IV

Part Two

LEVEL THREE VICTIMIZATION

Society's View/Victim Thinking

Victim thinking is acting as though you are still being assaulted. The rape is over, but it is still the dominant event in your life. You need not spend the rest of your life thinking like a victim. You can take control over your thoughts. A *martyr complex* is characteristic of victim mentality.

Continually focusing on your pain can lead to criticizing yourself and others. Emotional healing comes by speaking positive and encouraging words to yourself and others.

Here are a few victim thoughts:

- **Nobody will want me. I'm tarnished.**
- **I can't trust anyone anymore.**
- **I feel people are always looking at me, like "raped" is written on my forehead.**
- **The future scares me.**
- **I feel guilty.**
- **I will never get over this.**

We need to fight aggressively against victim thinking. You have the opportunity to make for yourself a productive, positive future. God has given you a chance to start over, to find a new identity, to view your world in a beautiful way you have never noticed before.

While rape is frightening, disgusting, and painful, it is not the end of the world. You are the same worthwhile, lovely person you were before. You do not have to be a marked-for-life victim. Choosing your own response allows you to stay in control and never be destroyed.

Now, say this out loud: "This is the last time I will ever think negative thoughts about myself. I choose to fight against victim thinking."

Society's View

Despite widespread media attention, reformed laws, and increased sensitivity, sexual assault remains an ambivalent issue in most people's minds. More often than not, the rape victim is seen as less than human. The unsympathetic see her as promiscuous or contaminated. It seems as if everyone is ashamed for her. Unlike any other victim of a violent crime, she is categorized as a failure for having been raped. People forget that rape is caused by the rapist, not the victim.[4]

People who view rape as sexual activity rather than violence believe that the rapist is motivated by uncontrollable desire, that the woman is somehow responsible for the attack, and that rape does not hurt the victim any more than sex does. They reason that it is not a cause for concern, but a subject to shun or to snicker about.[5]

Assignment: What is your opinion of society's view? Write down your thoughts.

_____

_____

_____

_____

_____

_____

_____

_____

_____

_____

_____

_____

_____

_____

_____

_____

ANNIVERSARIES

Anniversary dates can have a significant impact on people's behavior and emotional well-being. Concerns that survivors thought they had put to rest resurface. Many survivors re-experience Post-Traumatic Stress as the anniversary date of the trauma approaches.

Rape-related cues remind us of having been raped. The weather, holidays, and family celebrations are just a few. As these cues surface, recognize they are just cues—not an impending trauma (rape) about to happen. Your fear will subside, giving you control.

Your first anniversary may prove difficult, but with each passing year your anxiety will diminish. Every year you will discover new successes on which to focus. You will realize how far you have come in recovery, leaving you with sweet anticipation for the future.

Reclaim your anniversary date by connecting with someone and celebrate a new tradition.

Assignment: List some ways you can perceive this date in a positive way.

_____

_____

_____

_____

_____

_____

_____

TAKING CARE OF YOURSELF

Healing involves coming to terms with who you are, learning to see change not as an enemy but as an ally. When you can ask, "How can I find meaning in what has happened in my life?" change becomes possible. What happened in the past will not change; it will not become more beautiful or less ugly. But your feelings in the present—about yourself, about what happened, about what it all means—can change. Healing involves opening up new possibilities, new ways to be in the world that bring more peace inside.[6]

Taking good care of yourself means looking to many avenues of "stress release." Tears and laughter are super stress relievers. God gave us tears to wash away grief, anger, sorrow, and unanswered questions. Tears are God's way of helping us cope.

Tears help to keep our bodies free from disease and restore a sense of balance in our lives. William Shakespeare called our tears "holy water." So, for the sake of your health and your sanity, go ahead and have a good sacred sob once in a while.[7]

God replaces tears with laughter. That is His antidote to tears. When we laugh, our brains release a positive chemical reaction to naturally restore us. Churches have laughing seminars, and hospitals have laughing rooms—all value humor as healing.

> . . . put thou my tears into Thy bottle: are they not in Thy book?
>
> —Psalm 56:8 (KJV)

Here are more be-good-to-yourself comforts:

- **Enjoy tranquility.** Solitude at times can be lovely. Get up early to watch the sunrise. Prepare the night before by setting out a tray with a linen napkin and a nice cup and saucer. Prepare coffee or tea makings so all you have to do is plug in the pot. Set out fixings for cinnamon toast and fruit. Invite your dog or cat to join you. (They won't ruin the quiet by talking.) Then, in the morning, find a front-row seat and enjoy the free show. Or do the same for a sunset, enjoying dessert with the greatest video in the world!

- **Purchase humorous books on tape and/or videos.** Books on tape are wonderful. Just pop one in your car's cassette/CD player and let the humor tickle you all the way to work, the store, or wherever you're going. By the time you reach your destination, you'll feel quite chipper. Wind down with a comedy in the evening and your mind, body, and soul will be ready for a good night's sleep. If you need to go cheap, check them out from the library.

- **Take a break from the ordinary.** Rearrange your furniture. Cozy up that guest room and be a guest in it! Decorate for stress-free living: out with clutter, in with simplicity. Take the long way home (provided the scenery is nice).
- **Do something outrageous to relieve stress and anxiety.** Be on the lookout for mini miracles. Go to the drive-in movies in your jammies. Get a rubber ducky for your bathtub and play with it! Buy a pair of bright yellow or red rubber boots for rainy days, and stomp through water puddles with the neighbor kids. Learn a new "promise scripture" and tape it to your car's steering wheel. Believe that you are incredibly resilient—because you are! And live like you are!
- **Practice self-forgiveness.** Reject rejection. Smile when you don't want to. Confront conflict. Make mistakes so you can stretch. Eat an unfamiliar food item every month. Laugh out loud where strangers can hear you. Love yourself.
- **Play the "I Wish" game.** Check all of the following that you would wish for. Add a few of your own, and then make one come true.

I wish I could . . .

- ☐ buy a puppy/kitty
- ☐ take a two-day river cruise
- ☐ take a Chinese cooking class
- ☐ purchase season tickets to the theater or opera
- ☐ join a community theater house
- ☐ take riding/sailing lessons
- ☐ climb a mountain
- ☐ purchase a teddy bear

QUESTION TO ANSWER

What comfort did you do for yourself last week? Pick a new one for next week.

_____

_____

_____

_____

_____

_____

_____

_____

_____

_____

_____

WHAT ABOUT GOD?

"A sorrow that is shared is cut in half; a joy that is shared is doubled."

—St. Aelred of Rievaulx

"The Word of God has an amazing transforming capacity to renew and restore. Following the desolation of a sexual attack, your substance and stability can hinge on reading, meditating on, and memorizing meaningful Bible verses. Isaiah 26:3

promises 'You will keep in perfect peace him whose mind is steadfast, because he trusts in You.'

"If you have difficulty reading the Bible because you are still too angry or confused, Christian music, tapes, or literature can revive your spirit. However, some victims will need more time than others before they are open to any kind of spiritual nourishment." [8]

It is important to surround yourself with believers who can minister to you in prayer and comfort. "Two are better than one....If one falls down, his friend can help him up. But pity the man who falls and has no one to help him up!" (Eccl. 4:9-10).

Releasing Your Anger

Ephesians 4:26 says that emotional anger is not wrong; it's what we do with the anger that determines whether it is good or bad. It's normal at first to feel rage, hate, and bitterness toward the rapist. However, if these expressions continue, it will be destructive to your recovery. Instead of letting yourself get to the stage of exploding, share your feelings with an uninvolved party and with God.

One way of releasing pent-up anger is to "speak" to the rapist. Buried feelings surface when you can write in vivid detail about your sexual assault. Letter writing is a safe way of releasing bottled-up emotions of anger, bitterness, sadness, hate, fear and unforgiveness.

Assignment: Write a letter to your rapist. Tell him who you were before the rape, and how he changed your life after the rape. Express all the intensities of the emotions he left you with. Naming these emotions will help lead to healing and resolution. Take as much time as you need, in one sitting, or over a period of time.

This was my life and emotions before you turned it upside down:

_____

_____

_____

_____

_____

This is my life and emotions now:

_____

_____

_____

_____

_____

When you have finished your letter, you may either mail it to the rapist (yes, even if it was your father), throw it away, or tuck it in a drawer. I suggest you keep a copy to read in the future. You will be surprised at how much you have healed since the day you wrote it. There will come a time when you will read the letter and not feel any of the bitter emotions you once felt. You may want to bury or burn the original copy later as a final act of grieving. Congratulations! You are truly victorious!

MY PRAYER

Heavenly Father God,
I come before You once again with shaky feelings of fear, sad-
ness, and anger. Guide my hands as I write to the evil one
who shattered my life. Banish the shadows of hate. Clothe me
with forgiveness. Help me to see the perpetrator through the
eyes of Jesus that I might stand before You someday, grateful
for learning Your ways. Amen.

—L.R.S.

Assignment: Now, write a letter or poem of gratitude to God—
for creating you, for the special people in your life, for being
alive, for His presence, etc.

_____

_____

_____

_____

_____

_____

_____

_____

_____

_____

_____

_____

_____

_____

_____

_____

_____

_____

ONE WOMAN'S LETTER TO THE RAPIST

Bud,

I am writing this letter after much thought. I don't even know if you remember me. I am the young girl you raped and molested years ago. You and your wife were friends with my parents. In fact your wife was one of my mom's best friends.

It has taken years for me to deal with the issues of abuse you did. You took away my innocence and I resent that very much. I never felt like anyone would ever love me because of your acts of abuse; I have to tell you I hated you for that.

I hold you partially responsible for my marriage falling apart. I also blame you for the way I felt for years about who I was.

I have, however, come to a place where I understand that you are sick and need help. I pray that you have gotten help, and that you never did this to anyone else.

It is only by the grace of God and His healing in my life that I can write this letter without the hatred for you I had for years.

I am free, and I am not going to allow you to continue to hold me in bondage. May God bless your life and heal you of your own wounds.

—Chris

This letter to the rapist is a good start for the survivor. Hopefully, in time, she will come to forgive him.

YOU ARE RARE AND UNIQUE, O' WOMAN OF COURAGE!

CHAPTER 20

Women in Recovery from Rape

Session V

Part One

6:00   Prayer and humor
6:45   Read letters to the rapists
7:00   Rapist profiles (They Do It Because/All About Evil)
7:50   Break

Part Two

8:00   Emotional/spiritual growth
8:40   Taking care of yourself (It's a God thing)
8:55   Close

Prepare for next week: Bring humor to share.

Homework: Determine what to do with the letter to your rapist. Read Session VI.

Assignment: Write what forgiveness means to you.

Suggested Reading: *Forgive & Forget* by Lewis B. Smedes

He heals the brokenhearted and binds up their wounds.
—Psalm 147:3

Session V

Part One

THE EVIL SIDE OF MANKIND

What Is Evil?

Evil resides in the heart of everyone. We walk a fine line between the heart of a harlot and that of a saint. When mankind chooses to do harm, either through thoughts, words, or acts, he commits evil. Evil is a behavior; it is always a matter of choice. Evil is something inflicted on someone. "The heart is deceitful above all things and beyond cure" (Jer. 17:9).

Where Did Evil Come From?

To many minds, the origin of sin and the reason for its existence are a source of great perplexity. It is mysterious, unaccountable; to excuse it is to defend it. Could excuse for it be found, or cause be shown for its existence, it would cease to be sin. Lucifer was first of the covering cherubs, holy and undefiled, but little by little, he came to indulge a desire for self-exaltation . . . "I will exalt my throne above the stars of God: I will sit also upon the mount of the congregation . . . I will ascend above the heights of the clouds; I will be like the most High" (Isa. 14:13-14 KJV). The same spirit that prompted rebellion in heaven still inspires rebellion on earth; Satan induced man to sin.[1]

In Isaiah 14:12 Satan was referred to as the morning star and the son of the dawn. He was also called "the great dragon" and "that ancient serpent called the devil, or Satan, who leads the whole world astray" (Rev. 12:9). He was originally named Lucifer.

214

Satan, the deceptive, insidious arch criminal, has kept people blind to his far-reaching effects. Mankind has been dulled to his hideous and horrific atrocities. We can escape his influence and find safety in the arms of God.

When Did Evil Reveal Itself to Humankind?

Genesis of the Bible, the book of origins, reveals that evil began in the Garden of Eden. When God told Adam and Eve not to eat from the tree of the knowledge of good and evil, the serpent (Satan) tempted Eve. Both Adam and Eve ate of its fruit; thus sin entered in (Gen. 2:16-17). Heaven wept when Eden fell victim to sin, filling the world with woe.

All crimes and catastrophes can be traced to the wheel of evil that rolled down through the corridors of time. Lucifer's close relationship with the Creator made his crime even more atrocious. All the hopes of men and angels sank like rocks sinking to the bottom of the ocean.

As water reflects a face, so a man's heart reflects the man.
—Proverbs 27:19

RAPIST PROFILES

Mr. Roy Hazelwood, a retired FBI agent, gave the following information on the four types of perpetrators at his seminar entitled, Sexual Violence: Perpetrators and Victims (1997, Portland, Oregon).

Power Reassurance

This is the most common and least violent stranger-to-stranger rapist. He doesn't like what he is doing. His purpose is to reassure himself of his own masculinity. He is highly ritualistic, having no intent to punish or degrade his victim, and is verbally and sexually unselfish. He uses the surprise approach, with a minimal level of force, and pre-selects victims through window-peeping surveillance. The victim will be in his own age range, and he attacks between midnight and five A.M. He attacks victims in their own homes. The victim will remove her own clothing, and the sexual assault will take up a small portion of the time. He will most likely contact his victim again.

He has a low self-esteem, is an underachiever, non-athletic, solitary, takes little pride in appearance, collects non-violent pornography, works in a job with little contact with the public, and is unhappily married or in an unhappy relationship. This type can be treated.

Power Assertive

This is the second most common and third most violent. He is the date rapist. Very impulsive, he asserts his masculinity and feels it is his right to force women to have sex. He is verbally abusive, sexually selfish, uses the con approach, and exerts a moderate level of force. The victim will be in his own age range.

Assaults will take place away from where he lives or works. He will tear a victim's clothing off, rape the victim more than once, and rely on his fists for weapons. He wants to be viewed as a man's man. He is athletic, exercises regularly, drives a truck, may dress like a cowboy, loves to drink, and hangs out at bars. He takes pride in his personal appearance, is self-centered, and does not like authority figures. He will have a macho job, like construction, and will have multiple marriages. Successful treatment is marginal.

Anger Retaliatory

This is the third most common and second most violent. His purpose is to punish and degrade women, getting even for real or imagined wrongs. He is verbally abusive, sexually selfish, uses the blitz-style approach (sudden and violent), and uses excessive levels of force. The victim will be his age or older (but not the aged). He has no geographic or time pattern. He will rip/tear the victim's clothing off in the areas of assault, and he drinks prior to the assault. He has an explosive temper, abuses alcohol, and has a history of violence against women. He has a dark side, is a lone wolf and untrusting. He lacks a sense of humor, is a high school dropout, and has multiple marriages. Successful treatment is marginal.

Anger Excitation or the Criminal Sexual Sadist

These men are sexually aroused by the suffering of victims and need to have complete mastery over another person.

They use a con approach, carefully planning their assault and using advanced selection of location for the assault. They intentionally torture their victims, who will be strangers. They approach under a pretext in order to get a victim to participate. They beat their victim and keep them captive in sexual bondage. Tells the victim to speak in a degrading manner. Can be murderer/serial killer. Keeps personal items belonging to victims.

He is intelligent, and is the most manipulative, the biggest liar and boaster. He may be an established solid citizen, unemotional, unable to feel love. He is a sex dominant. He will become an expert on the subject, inflicting physiological and physical pain. His main preference is anal rape, and he maintains collections of violent themes.

217

His personality disorders include narcissism. He is grandiose, with a sense of entitlement, and is hypersensitive to criticism. He is antisocial. He shows no remorse, no capacity for empathy for others, no conscience, and cannot form lasting relationships. He is paranoid, suspicious, rigid, lacks humor, and puts the blame on others.

This is the least common and most violent, and he is untreatable.

QUESTION TO ANSWER

What profile did the one who raped you fit?

_____

_____

_____

_____

_____

_____

_____

_____

_____

_____

_____

_____

Session V

Part Two

EMOTIONAL/SPIRITUAL GROWTH

Do We Ever Recover?

For most of us, recovery is a gradual process. It moves silently, drawing us closer to peace every year. You may ask, "Will I ever recover? The answer is yes . . . you will recover. However, it's wishful thinking to set a time limit on your recovery. Everyone recovers differently. Recovery comes from maturing in our thinking, and a turn-around in our perception. Recovery comes by learning how to forgive, understanding evil, and the willingness to trust God for your recovery.

Recovery from rape can be a lifetime process. Just when we think we have recovered, something happens that rattles our cage. But we can reach out, take hold of the cage, and steady it. Remembering how far we have come will remind us of how far we can go.

Each individual is a unique human being graced with God's personal blueprint, unlike any other. Everyone perceives life differently, making reasoning our sole personal agenda. Perception is a key factor in recovery. Generally, it isn't the trauma itself that sends us in a spin, but our perception of it.

By allowing God to change your perception, you can learn to deal with intrusive negative thoughts of the past by replacing them with positive ones. This is where positive self-talk comes into play. Self-talk includes making a positive *choice* to heal.

CHOICES

ACCEPT. I choose to accept the fact that I cannot undo the reality of what has taken place in my life, but with God's help, I can change the *effect* it has on me.

AGREE. I choose to agree to live with the consequences of someone else's sin.

BELIEVE. I choose to believe that God's unfailing love for me can deliver me from all my wounds and strongholds.

CHANGE. Negative thinking leads to wrong behavior, producing rebellious actions. The consequences of my bad attitude can cause me to change my behavior if I allow God to show me.

DEAL. I choose to deal with past strongholds by letting go of anger, bitterness, contempt, and unforgiveness.

LISTEN. I choose to accept the past with an open heart by listening to God. Listening is being obedient.

FEAR NOT. I cannot eliminate the cause of fear, but I don't have to let it control me.

FORGIVE. I choose to relent to a teachable spirit and forgiving heart. Forgiveness is not for God; it is for me. It begins with a decision, a choice. The feeling that I have forgiven will follow, sooner or later.

TELL. I will tell my story, bringing hope and healing to others as well as myself.

Don't remain a victim. Choose to heal and become victorious. Making good choices, such as the ones above, will speed your recovery.

And yes, you will recover!

SIGNS OF HEALING

There are many signs that will indicate your recovery is coming along nicely. Many of your Post-Traumatic Stress symptoms will lessen as time passes. You will notice a reduced frequency of these symptoms. Your attitude will change from victim to survivor, and you will have a greater appreciation of life. Your sense of humor will increase. You will channel your anger and grief into something positive, and your sense of empathy will strengthen.

Other good signs are lack of suicidal thoughts, deriving some meaning from the trauma in your life, panic attacks lessening, being able to comfort yourself in a non-destructive way, and the confident growth of your self-esteem. You can learn to take this heinous trauma and turn it into a well of great strength.

QUESTION TO ANSWER

What signs indicate recovery coming closer for you?

_____

_____

_____

_____

_____

_____

_____

_____

RESOLUTION

In the resolution stage, your assault gradually loosens its power over you. You are less fearful, your anger has subsided, and you have ceased to blame yourself or others.

The resolution stage takes time. Do not consider yourself a failure if you feel you haven't "arrived." Let time run its course. Permit yourself to heal gradually. Remember, the more severe the assault, the greater the severity of your secondary wounding, and the less support you have from others, the more time it will take to heal.

TAKING CARE OF YOURSELF

Be Kind to Yourself.

Stop and consider your present life and how far you have come in your recovery. Count the ways: bravery, courage, higher self-esteem, a take-charge attitude, acceptance. Consider the ways you have let go of anger, bitterness, rage, sadness, and revenge. How about rewarding yourself with a five-minute retreat or a five-day retreat?

Here are some suggestions for be-good-to-yourself comforts.

- **Escape to faraway places in a children's book.** Search out your favorite children's books. Remember how your imagination took you off to another world? Well, you can return again and again. The enchantment and simplicity of children's books will bring peace and awe into your life.
- **Lift your spirits with dancing.** In spite of what you might think, everyone can dance. No, you don't have

to be a professional. Turn up the music and dance to your heart's content. It's hard to stay sad when you're dancing.

- **Play like a child.** Remember all the wonderful games you played as a child? Jacks, paper dolls, Tinkertoys, jump rope, hopscotch, tag, follow the leader, and hide and seek. Lose yourself in a toy store and surprise yourself with toys to bring home—and play with them!
- **Bed-and-breakfast in your own home town.** There is probably a bed-and-breakfast establishment just around the corner from your home. Or go to one out of town. If you're on a budget, see if you can stay in your best friend's guest room. The point is to indulge—sleep in someone else's bed, eat their food, dream and relax.
- **Commit yourself to healing.** It will come in layers, like a peeling sunburn. As each issue of your assault is dealt with, another layer of pain is peeled away. In its place will be the fresh, pink glow of peace.
- **Help others and yourself.** Sign up for a self-defense class. Volunteer to rock babies at your community hospital. Consider being an advocate (when you are ready) for your local sexual resource center.
- **Engage in positive self-talk.** Tell yourself, "I'm possible—not impossible." When you remove negative thoughts, you must fill your mind with positive ones. Scriptures are a good example.

Resolution does not remove the trauma.

It happened; it will not go away. Resolution is integration. As you mourn, make peace with acceptance, practice self-care, and take action to move on with your life, resolution takes hold.

Mourning Means Acknowledging and Experiencing What You Have Lost.

Grieving means feeling deep pain about what you have lost. It can be the loss of a loved one or the loss of physical capability. It can be the loss of a sense of safety in the world. It often is the loss of certain beliefs about the world.[2]

For a rape survivor, loss means many things in a hundred different ways. Each person is unique and perceptions vary. Mourning is painful but necessary in order to move on; it won't last forever.

Acceptance Means Accepting Your Loss.

We live in a fallen world where evil reigns. Bad things happen. Life isn't fair. But adversity strengthens us, instilling confidence to handle crises that may come our way. Despite the pain and devastation that comes with rape, those feelings can guide us toward maturity and inner healing. Something good will come of it.

Self-care Helps in Coping.

Self-care includes making your home and property safe, being careful who you are with (especially if you barely know them), and parking safely. These actions empower you; you are in charge. Go back to your normal routine as soon as possible; it crowds out mental intrusions.

Taking Action Is What You Are Doing Right Now.

You are seeking information that will enable you to recover from the effects of rape. Taking action is getting out of bed in the morning, getting dressed, and pursuing the plans of the day.

Taking action is talking to your medical doctor about anti-depressants if you suspect you would benefit from them. However, give careful consideration before starting such a program. Pills should only be used as a last resort, and for some people, not at all. Your doctor and counselor can help you with the pros and cons.

Above all, ask God what He would want you to do.

He has sent Me to heal the brokenhearted . . . to give them beauty for ashes, the oil of joy for mourning, the garment of praise for the spirit of heaviness.

—Isaiah 61:1-3 (NKJV)

IT'S A GOD THING

Don't Waste Your Sorrow.

There will always be evidence of scars resulting from our rape. Memories will linger in the depths of our souls. However, our scars can bear witness to God's unfailing love; He can create new life in us. Our brokenness can cause us to turn our wills and lives over to God. We can give Him our sorrow and trust that He will make us whole.

Lewis B. Smedes asks, in his book *Forgive and Forget,* "Will we let our pain hang on to our hearts where it will eat away our joy? Or will we use the miracle of forgiving to heal the hurt we didn't deserve?"[3]

Each individual is a unique human being, graced with God's personal blueprint, unlike any other. Everyone perceives life differently, making reasoning our sole personal agenda. Perception is a key factor in recovery. Generally, it isn't the trauma itself that sends us in a spin—it's our perception of it.

God can help you recover from having been raped. You can be free of the negative effect the rape has had on you. Ask

Him for new wings, and fly away from the strongholds that are keeping you grounded.

We each have a purpose in life. God has a plan for every one of us, and our reason for being is included in that plan. We are to use the pain that comes into our lives to help others overcome their pain; to give encouragement, hope, and love. As time passes and you seek and trust God, your reason for being will most likely be revealed to you.

"For I know the plans I have for you," declares the Lord, "plans to prosper you and not to harm you, plans to give you a future and a hope."

—Jeremiah 29:11

QUESTION TO ANSWER

What does forgiveness mean to you?

_____

_____

_____

_____

_____

_____

_____

_____

_____

MY PRAYER

Dear God,
Merciful Father God, as I accept my loss and mourn the past, help me see where You intervened. Enfold me with understanding. Replace sorrow with joy, and fill me with new love and strength that I may serve You and help others to heal. Amen.

—L. R. S.

YOU ARE A BRILLIANT DIAMOND, O' WOMAN OF COURAGE!

CHAPTER 21

Women in Recovery from Rape

Session VI

Part One

6:00　Prayer and humor
6:45　Forgiveness homework
7:00　Choosing to heal (forgiveness)
7:50　Break

Part Two

8:00　Taking care of yourself (have a good laugh)
8:15　Round Table Discussion
　　　(or watch a video, such as Chonda Pierce's *Girl's Night Out*)
9:30　Close

Suggested Reading: *Hinds' Feet on High Places* by Hanna Hurnard

You will go out in joy and be led forth in peace. . . .
Instead of the thorn bush will grow the pine tree,
and instead of the briars the myrtle will grow.

—Isaiah 55:12

Session VI

Part One

CHOOSING TO HEAL

Courtenay Harding of the University of Colorado asked survivors, "What really made the difference in your recovery?" Their answer: people who told them they had a chance to get better. Having belief in them translated into hope. Without hope, death can establish a foothold. Hope fights fear, and nurtures courage. It inspires vision and the work required to realize the unattainable.

"It isn't one person or incident or clinical intervention that is critical for change to occur. Instead, it's a complex process. One essential factor is keeping the spirit alive. Connecting with others helps; receiving respect and warmth breaks through the isolation, and helps you feel worth and alive" (*Psychology Today*, February 2001, p 39).

QUESTIONS TO ANSWER

Who is telling you that you have a chance to get better? Write down their names. If you can't think of anyone who is encouraging you, where can you go to keep your spirit alive? Write it down.

_____

_____

_____

What are you doing to break your isolation? List some ways.

_____

_____

Choosing to heal means going deep inside ourselves. It means we need to change our perception about our trauma. It means taking a hard look at our attitudes. It means we might have to consider forgiveness. It may be agonizing, temporarily. But healing will come. *Choosing* to heal is the first step to recovery.

When the psyche has been deeply wounded, the evil one marches in and starts a spiritual battle. He tries to smash our strength with weakness, keeping us defiant and defensive with others, and most of all, with God. This defiant, prideful contempt locks us into suffering and continues a pact with the devil. Beneath a veneer of contentment may be hidden despair pounding to get out, but it is locked in our hearts due to prideful stubbornness. Broken dreams and failed beginnings may appear to defeat us, but with Christ, they can never destroy us. However, they can reveal who we are.

Neil Anderson, Terry Zuehlke, and Julianne Zuehlke say in their book, *Christ Centered Therapy,* "Traumatic experiences contribute to the formation of the attitude. They are buried deep in our minds and they are what keep people in bondage to the past; not the traumatic experience itself. The difference is our perception. We cannot undo the reality of what has occurred in our lives, but we do have the power, with the Lord's help, to change the effect that the past may be having on us in current situations." [1]

We need to accept our past with an open heart. We need to push aside disappointments and sorrow in order for the healing path to begin. We need to trust God.

QUESTION TO ANSWER

What effects of having been raped are holding you in bondage? Write them down.

_____

_____

_____

_____

_____

_____

Anger

We cannot hang on to the past as an excuse for justifying our present anger. How does holding on to the past serve any positive purpose?

Confess your anger to God and ask Him to help you resolve it. You may have repressed anger or bitter feelings toward Him. You reason that if He is really God and truly benevolent, He wouldn't have allowed this to happen to one of His children. You may feel that God has abandoned you. In addition, you may think that a God who is most often characterized as male cannot understand a woman's victimization. His "maleness" makes Him an accomplice to the crime.[2]

While anger toward God is sometimes a normal reaction, it's always undeserving, since He claims in Psalm 103 to be perfectly fair, righteous, and loving in all that He does. He is never withdrawn or indifferent. In Isaiah 43:2 God promises to be with us in our suffering.

Confess your anger toward God (and others), and ask His help to resolve it; not for His sake, but for yours.[3]

QUESTIONS TO ANSWER

Identify your type of anger. Is it:

- Defiant/Prideful
- Contemptuous
- Defensive

Describe how your anger fits one of these categories (or one of your own). How does your anger act? How can you overcome anger?

_____

_____

How can you change the effects that having been raped has had on you?

_____

_____

What do you need to accept in order to recover?

_____

_____

To go beyond tolerable recovery, one must learn to deal with disappointments, sorrow, and trauma (even rape); not just cope with them. Here is the difference: Coping is like having a burr in your bed and figuring out ways to avoid it. Dealing with the burr is to remove it so you won't have to avoid it, thus giving you a good night's sleep.

Denial and excusing the severity of your wounds are not skills—they are crutches.

We break the strongholds of the rape by letting go of anger, bitterness, contempt, and unforgiveness. We embrace the past with acceptance and forgiveness, and anticipate something good will come of it. We let go and let God. This is dealing with it.

Kay Scott, author of the book *Sexual Assualt: Will I Ever Feel Okay Again?* said, "What do we do when we don't understand God's answers? Are we to say, 'God, You are unjust, maybe not righteous after all?' If we do that, then we remove ourselves from God's care; we wall ourselves out at the time of greatest need. We go through life cursing God and His people, rather than finding healing for our hearts even if we cannot gain understanding in our heads."[4]

MY PRAYER

Dear God,
I want to begin a new life. Help me turn contempt into contentment, and anger into acceptance. Grace me with a humble spirit, a forgiving heart, and the desire to remove my defiant, prideful attitude. Thank You for Your lovingkindness. Amen.

—L. R. S.

"I don't like this 'forgiveness' business," you say. "Why should I forgive? My rape tore away part of my life and I will never be the same. Even if I decided to forgive, I'm not ready."

I know just how you feel. But let's think about it.

Lewis B. Smedes said, "Forgiving does not reduce evil. Forgiving great evil does not shave a millimeter from its monstrous size. When we forgive evil we do not excuse it, we do not tolerate it, and we do not smother it. We look the evil full in the face, call it what it is, let its horror shock, stun and enrage us, and only then do we forgive it. If we say that monsters are beyond forgiving, we give them a power they should never have. They are given power to keep their evil alive in the hearts of those who suffered most."[5]

He added, "Forgiveness is God's invention for coming to terms with a world in which people, despite their best intentions, are unfair with each other and hurt each other deeply. He began by forgiving us. And He invites us all to forgive each other."[6]

Forgiving is not excusing or condoning. Forgiveness is not for God; it's for you—for you to be set free and feel the peace that surpasses all understanding, the kind only God can give. Until we forgive, we cannot entirely escape the strongholds of the pain and traumas in our lives.

Neil Anderson said, in his book *Christ-Centered Therapy*, "Forgiving is agreeing to live with the consequences of someone else's sin."[7]

Hardened hearts, pride, anger, and revenge block the path to forgiveness. God's original plan for humankind didn't include injustice, but due to sin, it happens. We can't escape it. We cannot forgive at the human level. Don't try to figure it out in the brain; you never will.

Forgiveness is not erasing the wrong of the rapist, nor do we forget when we forgive. It is a decision to accept the assault and let go of revenge. If you are stuck in a victim mentality, it's almost impossible to forgive. That's why it is important to move from a victim attitude to a victorious attitude.

A spirit of unforgiveness brings death to the soul, making spiritual recovery impossible. Forgiveness is not passive acceptance to let others stomp on us anytime they wish. It is a courageous act of the will.

Smedes said, "When we forgive, we perform a miracle hardly anyone notices. We do it alone, in the private place of our inner selves. We do it silently; no one can record our miracle on tape. We do it invisibly; no one can record our miracle on film. We do it freely; no one can ever trick us into forgiving someone."[8]

I cannot stand in judgment of those who choose not to do so. I just pray they will.

GOD REPAIRS AND RESTORES

Okay, now you have learned what forgiveness is and what it is not. Maybe you are ready to forgive. Let's give it a try. Whom do you *choose* to forgive?

If you feel you're not ready, name the main issue that is keeping you from doing so, such as revenge, anger, etc. Write it down.

If you are not ready to forgive, that's all right—for now. Forgiving is a process that takes time; it doesn't happen overnight. Ask God to help you forgive; it's the only way we can do it anyway.

Don't wait too long to make your choice to forgive. Hearts harden—you may never make the decision, thus eliminating your opportunity for wholeness. If you wish to wait for now, write God a letter or poem expressing your resistance, and ask Him to help.

MY PRAYER

Dear Heavenly Father,
I know You have forgiven me, and I in turn need to forgive.
But Father, the pain is still so deep, I can't move forward.
Guide me in the way of forgiving.
Help me to see others through Your eyes so I, too, will show mercy and have the courage to forgive. Amen.

—L. R. S.

Session VI

Part Two

TAKING CARE OF YOURSELF

"Time brings understanding and acceptance, so that living becomes meaningful again." [9]

Professional Help

If you are still having anxiety attacks, long crying spells, prolonged depression, and/or severe anger and rage, please seek professional help. You will not be seen as a "cry baby" or a weakling. It is a sign of taking care of yourself when you know you have tried everything and recovery is moving at a snail's pace. Seeking help is taking charge. Counseling can help you move toward recovery.

Join an Abuse Recovery Group

Listening and talking with others who have gone through the experience of rape can be very beneficial. You will feel safe when you share. A combination of individual and group therapy can be powerful.

Medication

Medical consultation should be sought if you are having sleep-related problems, depression, panic attacks, or overwhelming intrusions. Today's miracle drugs have few side effects and most are not addictive.

Most likely you will only need medication for a short time. However, medication without therapy won't help you resolve your trauma; neither will therapy alone help if you need the medication. Your doctor and therapist can help you make a decision.

HAVE A GOOD LAUGH AT YOURSELF!

"Humor is the sense of the absurd which is despair refusing to take itself seriously."

—*Arland Usshe*

Humor and laughter control pain in four major ways: (1) by distracting attention, (2) by reducing tension, (3) by changing expectations, and (4) by increasing production of endorphins—the body's natural painkillers. Laughter causes muscle relaxation and is effective when tension exists.[10] Humor and laughter can reduce emotional pain.

Laughter's mental effect is to break the fears that constitute the basis of so many depressions and lift one out of the black hole of despondency.

Humor as therapy can affect many things.

- **Humor has the power to reduce tensions and create a relaxed atmosphere.**
- **Humor puts an individual in a frame of mind conducive to constructive interchange with others.**
- **Humor can lead to insight into the cause of conflict and emotional disturbances.[11]**

We need periodic release from the obligation to be logical and serious about life's responsibilities. Humor allows us to deal in fantasy and nonsense and find respite from our serious cares and responsibilities.[12]

"Humor is reason gone mad."

—Groucho Marx

Peter's Prescription for Development of a Sense of Humor

- Adopt an attitude of playfulness.
- Think funny.
- Laugh at the incongruities in situations involving yourself and others.
- Only laugh with others for what they do rather than for what they are.
- Take yourself lightly.
- Make others laugh.

A sense of humor sees the fun in everyday experiences. It is more important to have fun than it is to be funny.[13]

QUESTIONS TO ANSWER

When was the last time you had a good belly laugh? Can you think of anything funny that happened to you this week? Write it (them) down.

_____

_____

_____

_____

_____

A cheerful heart is good medicine.

—Proverbs 17:22

HELP!

You might say, "I have gone through recovery programs. Why don't I feel healed? I expected big changes to take place."

Don't despair, you will recover from your sexual assault. Understanding your biochemistry and what you have learned in this book will form the basis for continued healing in the months ahead. The process of your healing will come gradually as you are able to change and adapt to a different you.

The ability to love, work, and play will be a good indicator that your recovery is taking place. Remember to focus on how far you have come and don't worry about the speed of your recovery. Hang in there—you'll make it!

I can do all things through Him who gives me strength.

—Philippians 4:13

MY PRAYER

Dear God,
I can't do it.
You can do it.
I don't know how.
I'll teach you.
Show me.
I am . . .

—*L. R. S.*

YOU ARE A SURVIVOR,
O' WOMAN OF COURAGE!

Joy Will Come in the Morning

God is the source of all comfort and healing. God, the Father of Jesus Christ, the Father of compassion, is the God who comforts us in all our troubles *so we can comfort those in trouble with the same comfort God gave us.*

He knows where we are in times of gladness and in times of sorrow. If we rise on the wings of the dawn or settle on the far side of the sea, He will guide us and hold us fast. When our life of suffering is over, we will be made new. God will wipe every tear from our eyes. There will be no more mourning, crying, pain, or death. Our present suffering is not worth comparing with the coming glory and what God has in store for us (See 2 Cor. 1:3-4; Ps. 139:10; Rev. 21:3-4).

Let God comfort you. Let Him heal you.

Dr. Dan B. Allender says, in his book *The Wounded Heart,* "You have been damaged. But you have great hope. The mercy of God does not eradicate the damage, at least not in this life, but it soothes the soul and draws it forward to a hope that purifies and sets free. Allow the pain of the past and the travail of the change process to create fresh new life in you and to serve as a bridge over which another victim may walk from death to life. It is an honor beyond compare to be part of the birthing process of life and hope, and a joy deeper than words to see evil and its damage destroyed. I await that day and joy with you."[14]

I, too, await that day and joy with you. What God did for me, He'll do for you.

Awesome blessings!

—Leila Rae

COVENANT WITH GOD

I agree to exchange fear, anger, unforgiveness, and bad choices for love and forgiveness. I will accept change, deal with perceptions, and relent to a teachable spirit. I accept the truth that good will come from bad. I believe God's unfailing love for me. I believe He can free me from past strongholds, thus guiding me to spiritual maturity and wholeness. With God, I believe "awful" is not forever, and that "awesome" will dwell in its place. I will tell my story of healing to others.

_____

Signature   Date

SUMMARY

STEPS TO WHOLENESS

- Make the choice to heal.
- Allow God to change your perception.
- Let people help; don't isolate yourself.
- Feast on the Word of God.
- Tell your story to a trusted person, get counseling, or both.
- Release your anger, bitterness, contempt, and rage. Write a letter to those who hurt you.
- Find safety in God. Write Him a letter about your hurt.
- Write a letter to yourself from God, having Him console you.
- Mourn. Bring your grief to Jesus; let Him comfort you.
- Agree to live with the consequences of someone else's sin.
- Take good care of yourself.
- Forgive yourself.
- Forgive others.
- Laugh.

RESOURCES FOR RAPE SURVIVORS AND THOSE WHO CARE ABOUT THEM

FACTS TO REMEMBER

FACT: Rape is a crime of power and control, anger and violence. It is not a crime of passion.

FACT: Survivors did not provoke their rape. The perpetrators were responsible.

FACT: Sexual assault is everyone's problem. We must speak out and break the silence, challenging the social and cultural traditions that nurture it.

FACT: Rape is a crime against the state as well as the survivor.

A GUIDE FOR HUSBANDS, FATHERS, AND FRIENDS

A rape survivor is confused, anxious, and emotionally charged immediately following her rape. She has been terrorized, violated, and is faced with many worries and questions such as:

- **Should I report this to the police?**
- **Could I be pregnant?**
- **Have I contacted venereal diseases or AIDS?**
- **What will my family, husband, and others think of me?**
- **Will I ever be the same as before my rape?**
- **Do I need to see a doctor?**
- **Will he try to rape me again?**

The emotional aftermath of rape continues well beyond the assault. Encouraging her to seek medical attention and counseling sends a powerful message that you believe her and view her assault seriously. She will feel your support, knowing she will not have to face her recovery alone.

Because the time following her rape is filled with psychological forces, great sensitivity and care must be taken. How you communicate with her is critical. It will determine her self-worth and how she feels about herself. Those closest to her have the honor and power to help her recover.

How Can You Help?

1) Never accuse or judge her. Don't ask questions such as, "Why didn't you scream for help? Why were you there after dark? Why did you wear that outfit?" Such questions will only make her feel guilty.

2) When a woman has been raped, she feels a loss of control over her life. In order to help her regain a sense of control, she should be encouraged to make her own decisions (e.g., whether to report the crime, go to trial, etc.).

3) Don't demand details of her rape. Be patient. When she is ready to discuss it, she'll let you know.

4) She needs to feel your love and know that it will remain intact, that you will endure this crisis together, no matter what happened or will happen later.

5) Eventually, you must discuss the impact the rape has had on your relationship. The aftermath of rape is traumatic for everyone involved with her, especially if you are her father, boyfriend, or husband. Nurturing your loved one will speed her recovery.

6) Don't joke about or trivialize her rape.

7) Don't overprotect the survivor. It can discourage her from finding coping skills. This can promote dependency on others. Help her be independent by supporting her.

8) Don't smother her. Accept her need for privacy. It's desirable and therapeutic for her to work alone with her feelings. Well-wishers can drain her emotionally.

9) Take any suicide threat seriously. Notify her family and counselor immediately.

Here are more ways you can help:

A rape survivor needs a safe, accepting climate in order to release painful feelings, free of criticism. Being patient, supportive, and nonjudgmental will send her an important message . . . that you love her unconditionally. You can help by just being there. Listen, listen, listen.

Protect yourself when you enter into another's pain; it can engulf you. Acknowledge your own inadequacies. You cannot make it better—you have no solutions or answers. Encourage her to seek professional help.

Don't minimize the assault by saying, "At least you weren't murdered!"

Don't excuse the perpetrator. Assure her the rape was not her fault; there is never an excuse for rape. And for heaven's sake, don't suggest the rape might not have happened if she had prayed harder.

Don't give up on her. Stay for the long haul, because healing is a long process, a lifetime process. Don't expect her to fight all by herself. The soul's enemy (Satan) desires to destroy her. She is in a spiritual battle. Pray for her. Let her know you have faith that her healing will come, because in the midst of her darkness, her faith is dead. Phone occasionally and send notes of encouragement. Invite her to do something fun.

You will find great joy in participating in the restoration of a survivor.

BE A SAMARITAN: CARE FOR A WOMAN'S SOUL

Larry Crabb says, in his book *Connecting,* "Ordinary people have the power to change other people's lives. The power is found in connection, that profound meeting when the truest part of one soul meets the emptiest recesses in another and finds something there, when life passes from one to the other. The power to meaningfully change lives depends not on advice . . . but on connecting, on bringing two people into an experience of shared life.

"We were designed to connect with others; connecting is life . . . tears without an audience, without someone to hear and care, leave the wounds unhealed. When someone listens to our groaning and stays there, we feel something change inside us. Despair seems less necessary; hope begins to stir where before there was only pain.

"Connecting begins when we enter the battle for someone's soul. It continues as we prayerfully envision what Christ would look like in that person's life. It climaxes when the life of Christ within us is released, when something wonderful and alive and good pours out of us to touch the heart of another."[15]

You can care for the souls of those who have been sexually assaulted. If you have been healed, don't waste your sorrow—help others. Throw them a safety net. Enter into the relationship of soul care. Lead a recovery class and/or make yourself available one-on-one. Shepherd a woman's heart—become a Samaritan.

> But a certain Samaritan . . . had compassion on [her], and went to [her], and bound up [her] wounds, pouring in oil and wine, and set [her] on his own beast.
>
> —Luke 10:33-34 (KJV)

LETTER TO DAUGHTER
FROM GOD

Dear Daughter,

You've lived in darkness long enough. It's time to put on the armor of light. You are ready to soar like an eagle. Leave sorrow behind. Cast off the chains of fear. Cast off your strongholds. Don't dwell on past mistakes and sorrow.

I'm doing new things in you now. I am healing your broken heart and binding your wounds. I know you don't perceive it now, but as they spring up, your life will transform, and then you will feel My hand upon you.

Don't let evil overcome you. Do good things, overcoming evil with good. I am restoring your health. I am restoring your sanity. I am showering you with peace and prosperity. You will not be afraid anymore. You will dwell in safety and your sleep will be sweet.

I am the God of Comfort. I am the Lord, who heals you. Your soul will be filled with joy, and peace will lead you. I am healing your wounds of thorns and briars. I anoint your spirit with roses and lilies. Come away, My beloved. Let Me continue to heal you.

—God

IF YOU HAVE BEEN RAPED
OR SEXUALLY ASSAULTED

Call 911 for help and call a trusted friend, relative, or church leader.

Do not change your clothes (they will be needed for evidence), bathe, brush your teeth, or straighten up the assault area.

Go to the emergency room of a hospital as soon as possible unless the police ask you to wait for them. In that case, they will escort you to the hospital. If you were raped in an unsafe area, let the police know.

When you arrive at the hospital, most likely an advocate from a sexual assault center will be there for you; you won't be alone. Exams are important to detect injury and inform you of your options regarding pregnancy and protection from sexually transmitted diseases. The state will pay for your exam if police are notified.

Reporting the crime may make you eligible for compensation for medical/counseling costs or losses associated with the crime. Rape is a crime against the state.

Reporting the crime will also give you a sense of control, and the information you offer may help prevent the attacker from assaulting again.

Seek counseling, preferably with someone who works with sexual assault survivors.

Attend a sexual assault recovery support group. Ask if your church has one.

Call for information on rape crisis services in your community, or check your telephone directory, mental health clinics, local hospital, or police department. Some nonprofit mental health clinics and churches provide counseling for those unable to pay.

National Rape Crisis Hotline: 1-800-656-4673

Post this flyer in public restrooms and on bulletin boards at places such as libraries, churches, and schools.

QUESTION EVALUATION FORM

How do you feel about the group ending? Would you like it to be longer?

_____

How has attending this group helped you?

_____

Was the information given clear? If not, what didn't you understand, and how could this program be more helpful?

_____

_____

_____

What part of the recovery program would you like to learn more about, or what do you feel was left out?

_____

_____

_____

Please rate instructor(s)	Poor	Fair	Good	Excellent
Please rate program				

Leave with leader, signed or unsigned. Your opinion will help improve future programs. Thank you.

PERMISSION TO USE CONFIDENTIAL INFORMATION IN A PUBLIC FORUM

I hereby give permission to use the information disclosed in the Taking Back Control class in public forum for the purpose of demonstration, testimonial, instruction, and training. I do not limit this disclosure in any form except for the limitations listed below. This information can be communicated in public speaking, written materials, recorded media, or any other means that benefit the purposes of the one given permission.

The following limits are to be applied to the above permission granted:

- **The use of my real name is prohibited.** _____ (initial)
- **Cannot use descriptive statements that reveal my identity.** _____ (initial)
- **Other:**

Signature _____ Date _____

Witness _____ Date _____

* SAMPLE FLYER *

TAKING BACK CONTROL

WOMEN IN RECOVERY
FROM THE AFTERMATH OF RAPE
&
GUIDANCE FOR THOSE WHO WANT TO HELP

LEARN ABOUT

THE THREE LEVELS OF VICTIMIZATION
POST-TRAUMATIC STRESS
RECONSTRUCTING YOUR LIFE
ASSERTIVENESS & SAFETY
MYTHS ABOUT RAPE
EMOTIONAL & SPIRITUAL GROWTH
TAKING CARE OF YOURSELF
WHERE IS GOD IN ALL OF THIS?
COPING SKILLS
IS INCEST RAPE?
JOURNEY TO WHOLENESS

WHERE: Canby New Life Foursquare Church, 2350 Territorial Rd., Canby, Oregon. Bldg. #5 upstairs

WHEN: May 20-22, 2004 (No child care or classes)

TIME: Thurs. & Fri. 6:00 P.M. to 9:00 P.M. *Sat. 9:00 A.M. to 4:00 P.M.

COST: $25 (includes book)

CLASS SIZE LIMITED
APPLICANTS MUST PRE-REGISTER

This is a closed, confidential class and will not be open after class starts. Applicants must be over 16 years of age (parental consent if minor). To register, call Jane Doe at (123) 123-4567.

The night is far spent, the day is at hand:
let us therefore cast off the works of darkness,
and let us put on the armour of light.

—Romans 13:12

253

PROFESSIONAL DISCLOSURE STATEMENT

A biblical approach is taken in leading and ministering to the needs of the whole person, reflecting the love, mercy, and healing power of the Holy Spirit. Women in recovery from sexual assault (of any kind) are provided a safe, confidential place to share and work together for the healing of everyone. Our mission is to instill courage to heal from sexual wounds and confidence to grow spiritually and emotionally.

Name _____ Phone Number (___)_____

Address _____

Signature _____ Date _____

E-mail_____

Cost: $25. Applicants must be over sixteen years of age (parental consent if minor).

*Please bring a sack lunch for Saturday class. Beverage and dessert will be provided.

SAMPLE
REGISTRATION * AGREEMENT

TAKING BACK CONTROL
WOMEN IN RECOVERY
FROM THE AFTERMATH OF RAPE

Participants in Women in Recovery from Rape class agree to the following:

- I will attend all meetings, be on time, and contact group leader if unable to attend.
- I will let the leader know if I am unable to finish the class.
- I understand that first names only are to be used. No cross talking, which takes away full attention and respect from the leader. No children or unauthorized visitors are allowed in class. No tape recording. No disclosure of any group member to outsiders. No substance abuse on day of meeting.
- Leader has the authority to remove any participant from the group if deemed necessary in order to maintain the integrity of the group.

SUGGESTED READING

- **New Beginnings: Daily Devotions for Women Survivors of Sexual Abuse,** (Thomas Nelson Publisher, Nashville, 1992). Out of print but worth looking for.
- **Hinds' Feet on High Places,** Hannah Hurnard. (Wheaton, IL: Tyndale, 1977). An allegory of hope and courage when faced with fear.
- **Recovery from Rape,** Linda E. Ledray, (New York: Henry Holt & Co., 1986). In-depth information about rape and how to recover.
- **Shattering Your Strongholds,** Liberty Savard, (New Jersey: Bridge Logos, 1992). How to break strongholds.
- **The Wounded Heart,** Dr. Dan B. Allender, (Colo. Springs, CO: NavPress, 1990). For adult survivors of childhood sexual abuse. A must read for incest survivors.
- **Boundaries,** Dr. Henry Cloud and Dr. John Townsend., (Grand Rapids, MI, Zondervan, 1992). When to say yes, when to say no. Learn to take control of your life.
- **On the Threshold of Hope,** Diane Mandt Langberg, Ph.D., (Wheaton, IL: Tyndale, 1999). Healing sexual abuse. A gentle book full of hope and God's grace.
- **Forgive and Forget,** Lewis B. Smedes, (N.Y: Pocket Books, 1984). How to forgive.
- **Forgiving Our Parents: Forgiving Ourselves,** Dr. David Stoop and Dr. James Masteller, (Ann Arbor, MI: Zondervan, 1991). Forgive your parents so you can forgive yourself.
- **Invisible Wounds,** Candace Walters (Portland, OR, Multnomah Press, 1987) God's Way of Healing from Rape.

Endnotes

NOTES

Part I Beyond Our Control – Rape: My Story

Chapter 1: *Nighttime Intruder*

1. Judith S. Wallerstein, Julia M. Lewis, Sandra Blakeslee, *The Unexpected Legacy of Divorce* (N.Y.: Hyperion, 2000), 240, 241.
2. Frederick Buechner, *Godric* (N.Y.: Atheneum, 1981), 51.
3. Linda E. Ledray, R.N. Ph.D., *Recovery From Rape* (New York: Henry Holt & Co., 1986), 10.
4. Ibid., 13.
5. Ibid., 231.
6. Nancy Vanable Raine, *After Silence* (N. Y.: Crown, 1998), 80.
7. Ibid., 80.

8. Willard Gaylin, M.D., *Adam & Eve & Pinocchio* (N.Y., NY: Viking Penguin, 1990), 85.

9. Herbert Wagemaker, M.D., *The Surprising Truth about Depression* (Grand Rapids, MI: Zondervan, 1994), 123.

10. *Psychology Today* (February 2001), 39.

11. Thomas Moore, *Care of the Soul* (N.Y., NY: Walker & Co., 1992), 38.

Chapter 2: *The Ladies' Tree*

1. Willard Trask, *Joan of Arc, in Her Own Words* (N.Y.: Turtlepoint Press, 1996), 4, 5.

2. Janet Valenta Allen, *Out of Madness*, (Beaverton, OR: Good Samaritan Ministries, 1993), 16.

3. Ledray, 103, 104, 105.

4. Sean Mactire, *Malicious Intent* (Cincinnati, OH: Writer's Digest, 1995), 30.

5. George Johnson, *In the Palaces of Memory* (N.Y.: Alfred A. Knopf, 1991) xi, xiv, 230, 232, 233.

6. Frederic Buechner, *Telling Secrets* (San Francisco: Harper, 1991), 30, 31.

7. Cullen Murphy, *The Word According to Eve* (Boston, N. Y.: Houghton Mifflin Co., 1998), 52.

8. Ibid., 4.

9. Jim Conway, *Adult Children of Divorce* (Downers Grove, IL: InterVarsity, 1990), 63.

10. Wallerstein, 27, 37.

Chapter 3: *The Nutcracker Suite*

1. Allen, 133.

2. Haines & Haggy, *The Pathway of Life* (Chicago, IL: Elder & Co., 1882), 215.

3. Leonard Shengold, M.D., *Soul Murder* (Columbine, N.Y.: Fawcett Books, 1989), 3.
4. Ibid., 24.
5. Wagemaker, 177.
6. Mactire, 134.
7. Ibid., 134, 138.
8. Raine, 61.

Chapter 4: *His Name is Crackers*

1. Dominic Bosco, *Bedlam* (N.Y., NY: Carol Publishing 1992), 316.
2. Allen, 70.

Chapter 6: *The Loud, Silent Year*

1. Neil Anderson, Terry Zuehlke & Julianne Zuhlke, *Christ Centered Therapy* (Grand Rapids, MI: Zondervan, 2000), 156.
2. Ibid., 97.
3. Lewis B. Smedes, *Forgive & Forget* (N.Y.: Pocket Books, 1984), 107.
4. Ibid., 12.
5. Ibid., 141.
6. Debbie Morris, *Forgiving the Dead Man Walking* (Grand Rapids, MI: Zondervan, 1998), 249, 251.
7. Liberty Savard, *Shattering Your Strongholds* (New Jersey: Bridge Logos, 1992), 90.

Chapter 8: *Tough Love*

1. Gavin DeBecker, *The Gift of Fear* (N.Y., NY, Dell, 1997), 56.

Chapter 9: *Facing the Enemy*

1. Allen, 37.

Chapter 10: *Do We Ever Recover?*

1. Smedes, 21.
2. Bruce Larson, *Living Beyond Our Fears* (N.Y., NY: Harper Row, 1990), 150.
3. Louis Palau, *Where Is God When Bad Things Happen?* (N.Y.: Doubleday, 1999), 215, 216.

Part II A Biblical, Historical and Social Perspective about Rape

Chapter 11: *Mother Eve*

1. *The Wycliffe Commentary,* King James (Chicago: Moody Press, 1962), 1.
2. *Matthew Henry Commentary,* NIV (Grand Rapids, MI: Zondervan, 1992), 1.
3. *The History of Women, Vol. III* (Cambridge, MA: First Harvard Press, 1993), 447.
4. *The History of Women, Vol. II* (Cambridge, MA: First Harvard Press, 1992), 363, 366.
5. Ibid., 362.
6. Ibid., 36, 37.
7. Ibid., 34, 35.
8. *Wycliffe*, 5.
9. *Matthew Henry Commentary,* 7.
10. Wycliffe, 6.
11. *The History of Women, Vol. III*, 447.
12. Ibid., 21.
13. *The History of Women, Vol. II*, 21.
14. Ibid., 13.

15. *Wycliffe*, 5.
16. Ellen G. White, *The Great Controversy Between Christ & Satan* (Mt. View, CA: Pacific Press Pub., 1888), 541.

Chapter 12: *They Do It Because They Want To*

1. Mactire, 32.
2. Ibid., 34.
3. Ibid., 34.
4. Ibid., 34.
5. Ibid., 25.
6. Ibid., 25.
7. Ibid., 25.
8. Ibid., 2.
9. Ibid., 6.
10. Ibid., 31.
11. Liz Kelly, *Surviving Sexual Violence* (Minneapolis: University of Minnesota Press, 1988), 199.

Chapter 13: *Our Fathers' Iniquities*

1. *Rodale Synonym Finder* (Emmaus, PA: Rodale Press, 1978) 106.

Chapter 14: *The Ties That Bind*

1. *The History of Women, Vol. II*, 1.
2. Ibid., 161.
3. Ibid., 135.
4. *The History of Women, Vol.1* (Cambridge, MA: First Harvard Press, 1992), 409.
5. Merlin Stone, *When God Was a Woman* (New York: Double Day, 1976), 226.
6. Ibid., 226.
7. Ibid., 226.

8. *The History of Women Vol. I*, 428.
9. Ibid., 451.
10. Rachel Biale, *Women & the Jewish Law* (Brooks, N.Y.: Schocken, 1984), 27.
11. History of Women, Vol. II, 101.
12. History of Women, Vol. I, 417.
13. *NIV Holy Bible* (Grand Rapids, MI: Zondervan, 1985), 271, 272.
14. Sandra Mackey, *Saudis – Inside the Desert Kingdom* (N.Y., NY: Signet, 1990), 173.
15. Ibid., 133.
16. Ibid., 135.
17. Ibid., 137.
18. Ibid., 140.
19. *The History of Women Vol. II*, 56.
20. *The History of Women Vol. II*, 308.
21. Ibid., 277.

Chapter 15: *Dear Church*

1. Candace Walters, *Invisible Wounds* (Portland, OR: Multnomah Press, 1987), 116, 117, 118.
2. Ibid., 87.

Part III Taking Back Control: Restructuring Your Life after Rape, and Guidance for those Who Want to Help.

Chapter 16: *Women in Recovery from Rape – Session I*

1. Eddie Ensley & Robert Hermann, *Writing to be Whole* (Chicago: Loyola Press, 2001), x.
2. Louise De Salvo, *Writing as a Way of Healing* (San Francisco, CA: Harper Collins, 1999) 25.

3. Vicki Aranow & Monique Lang, *Journey to Wholeness* (Florida: Learning Pub., 2001), 114.
4. Walters, 47.
5. Aphrodite Matsakis, *I Can't Get Over It* (Oakland, CA: New Harbor Press, 1996), 85.
6. Mariann Hybels-Steer, Ph.D., *Aftermath* (N.Y., NY: Fireside Pub., 1995), 29.
7. Ibid., 35.
8. Ensley & Hermann, 7.
9. Walters, 86.

Chapter 17: *Women in Recovery from Rape – Session II*

1. Benjamin Colodzin Ph. D., *How to Survive Trauma* (Barrytown, N.Y.: Station Hill Press, 1992), 1, 2.
2. Diane Langberg, Ph.D., *On the Threshold of Hope* (Wheaton, ILL: Tyndale, 1999), 108.
3. Colodzin, 87.
4. Arranow, 75.
5. Walters, 88.

Chapter 18: *Women in Recovery from Rape – Session III*

1. Colodzin, 19, 20.
2. Ibid., 20, 21.
3. Aranow, 114.
4. Walters, 89, 97.

Chapter 19: *Women in Recovery from Rape – Session IV*

1. Colodzin, 33, 34.
2. Ibid., 34, 35.

3. Ibid., 36, 37.
4. Walters, 26.
5. Ibid., 29.
6. Colodzin, 14.
7. Sue Augustine, *5-Minute Retreats for Women* (Eugene, OR: Harvest Pub., 2001), 72.
8. Walters, 90.

Chapter 20: *Women in Recovery from Rape – Session V*

1. White, 492, 494, 500.
2. Hybels-Steer, 108.
3. Smedes, 21.

Chapter 21: *Women in Recovery from Rape – Session VI*

1. Anderson/Zuhlke, 97.
2. Walters, 95.
3. Ibid., 96.
4. Kay Scott, *Sexual Assault: Will I Ever Feel Okay Again?* (Grand Rapids, Bethany House, Division of Baker Pub. Group, 1993), 103.
5. Smedes, 107.
6. Ibid., 112.
7. Anderson/Zuhlke, 156.
8. Smedes, 1.
9. Dr. Laurence J. Peter, *The Laughter Prescription* (N.Y., Ballantine Books, 1982), 88.
10. Ibid., 8.
11. Ibid., 77.
12. Ibid., 56, 88.
13. Ibid., 193.

14. Dr. Dan Allender, *The Wounded Heart* (Colo. Springs, CO: NavPress, 1990), 263.
15. Larry Crabb, *Connecting*, (Nashville, TN, Word Pub., 1997), 31, 53, 127, 170.

CONTACT THE AUTHOR

For more information about leading/teaching seminars for women in recovery from the aftermath of rape, you may e-mail Leila Rae Sommerfeld at *leilarae@centurytel.net*
Website: leilaraesommerfeld.com

To order additional copies of

Beyond Our Control–*Rape*

Have your credit card ready and call toll free:

1-877-421-READ (7323)

or please visit our web site at
www.pleasantword.com

Also available at:
www.amazon.com
www.barnesandnoble.com
and
www.christianbook.com

Printed in the United States
50657LVS00004B/199-282